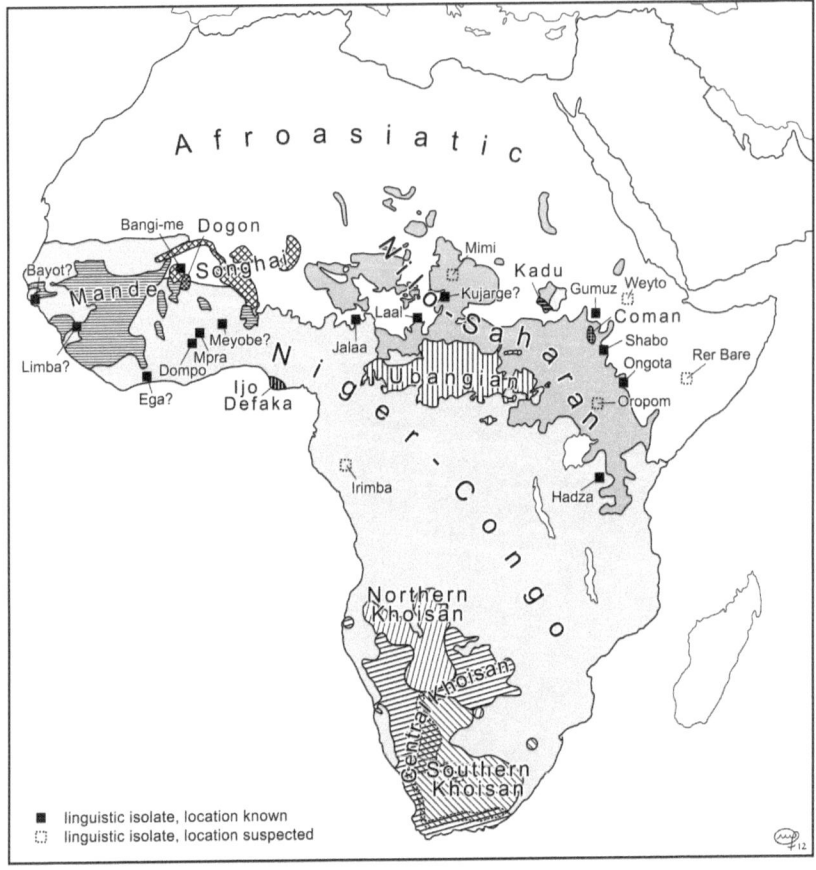

Map of the territories where the Niger-Congo linguistic continuum resides and where its influence resounds most distinctly, alongside the neighboring continua with which it has been most immediately and profoundly co-articulated and reciprocally shaped. This book is grounded in the argument that this continuum is not merely linguistic, but also rhythmic and psychic—proposing that language, rhythm, and psychology are co-articulated dimensions of collectivity. Though the linguistic dimensions were systematically repressed, the rhythmic and psychic dimensions have endured among Africans in the New World—having passed through the Door of No Return, survived the Middle Passage, and resisted the ethnocidal machinery of racial capitalist slavery and the assimilative forces of Western "civilization." These rhythmic and psychic dimensions have transformed European languages, giving rise to Black vernaculars.

MUINDI FANUEL MUINDI

FUGITIVE EROTICS
BLACK RITES OF BREAKAGE AND REPAIR

solutionsforpostmodernliving.org

Fugitive Erotics: Black Rites of Breakage & Repair
First edition: June 20, 2025
© 2025, Muindi Fanuel Muindi
© 2025, solutionsforpostmodernliving

ISBN: 979-8-218-65860-1
Printed by solutionsforpostmodernliving

Cover image courtesy of Letaru Dralega
Dust, 2021
Oil, spray paint& 24ct goldleaf on canvas

CONTENTS

Preface: From Social Realism to Post-Social Surrealism............... 7

PRELIMINARY ESSAYS

A Black Planet 14
A Lesson in the Black Arts & Decolonial Sciences 28

FUGITIVE EROTICS

Introduction: Desire at the Crossroads......................................66
The Sub-Molecular: The Sensual..74
The Molecular: The Relational..80
The Molar: The Systemic 96
The Colonial Order of Sexuality: An Outline........................... 106
Fugitive Erotics: Kinship in Resistance.................................... 122
The Break: Chicago House 140
Bass Materialisms, Maroon Choreographies, Sonic Ecologies . 168
Black Planetary Futures.. 188

Postscript: Giving New Flesh to Old Wounds......................... 194

Map from the UNESCO Slave Routes Project depicting the estimated 24 million people kidnapped and deported from Africa between the 8th and 19th centuries—primarily peoples of the Niger-Congo linguistic, psychic, and rhythmic continuum—alongside the continent's estimated 19th-century population of 100 million, and a projected population of 200 million had the transatlantic slave trade not taken place.

To borrow from AbdouMaliq Simone (2004): people are infrastructure. Few understand this more intimately than Afro-diasporic peoples—both those violently uprooted, kidnapped, exported overseas, and subjected to slavery and social death beyond the continent, and those who remained, surviving in the wake of these apocalyptic disappearances. These disappearances were not merely the destruction of peoples but the devastation of infrastructures—trade routes severed, governance systems dismantled, architectures of knowledge and relation razed.

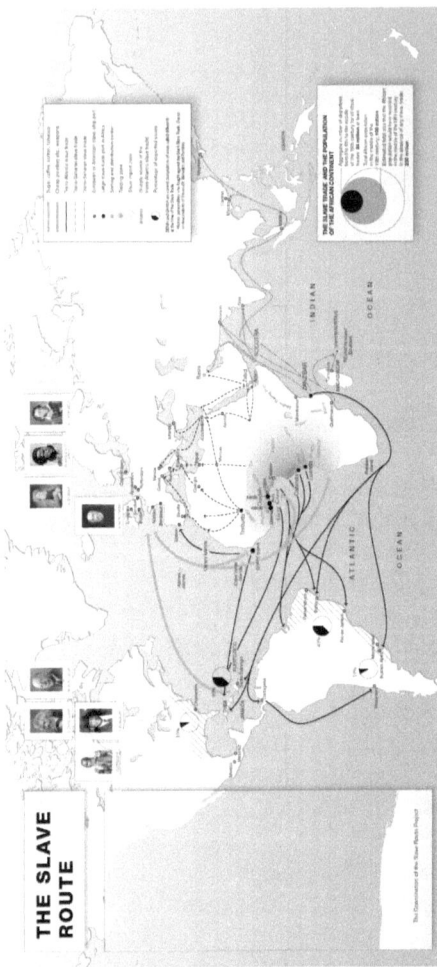

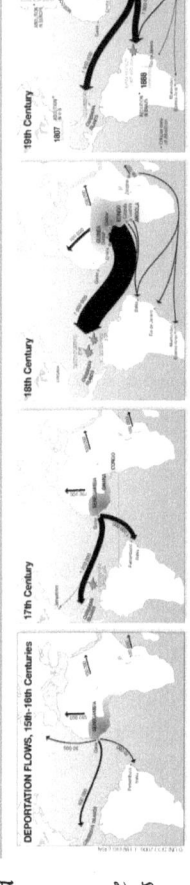

PREFACE
From Social Realism to Post-Social Surrealism

"Now, the following are truths which a knowledge of the history of the world, and particularly of that of our own country, compels us to know — that the African negro race never has been acknowledged as belonging to the family of nations; that among them there has never been known or recognized by the inhabitants of other countries anything partaking of the character of nationality, or civil or political polity; that this race has been by all the nations of Europe regarded as subjects of capture or purchase, as subjects of commerce or traffic; and that the introduction of that race into every section of this country was not as members of civil or political society, but as slaves, as property in the strictest sense of the term."

— Justice Daniels, Concurring Opinion, Dred Scott v. Sandford (1857)

The above remarks from the infamous Dred Scott case are not an aberration. They reflect a prevailing worldview at the time—one echoed by many of Western civilization's most revered philosophers: Hume (the empirical), Kant (the critical), Hegel (the dialectical), and Heidegger (the phenomenological), among them.

According to this logic, for the "African negro" to gain recognition or freedom, they must prove themselves to be more than property—more than tools, machines, or commodities; more than fleshy organs to be harvested and put to use. They must demonstrate that they belong to the "family of nations," that they are competent members of a legitimate civil or political society. To the extent that African descended peoples still find themselves needing to prove this, again and again, times have not changed as much as we might like to think.

But who defines what it means to belong to this family? Who sets the terms of recognition? If it is the European, then the African must first demonstrate the capacity to socialize in ways the European is willing to acknowledge—on terms not of their own making.

Social realists among the African diaspora often find themselves caught in this bind. Some strive to prove they can do civilization on European terms. Others attempt to redefine those terms through discourse—seeking participation in civilization without being absorbed by it, without becoming Westernized. Some go further still, asserting the "African Origin of Civilization" to claim legitimacy on their own historical ground.

Post-social surrealists[1] of the diaspora, by contrast, reject the premise entirely. They know that African peoples are capable of conforming to European standards of civilization. They know they can engage in discourse to reshape the terms. They are well aware of the African origin of civilization. But they simply don't believe they should have to prove themselves anymore—and they don't care to. Following Toni Morrison, they recognize that the racist logic underpinning this double bind is, above all, a distraction:

"The function, the very serious function of racism is distraction. It keeps you from doing your work. It keeps you explaining, over and over again, your reason for being. Somebody says you have no language and you spend twenty years proving that you

---

1   The distinction I draw between social realism and post-social surrealism is informed by a passage from Kodwo Eshun's *More Brilliant Than the Sun* (1998): "Everywhere, the 'street' is considered the ground and guarantee of all reality, a compulsory logic explaining all Black Music, conveniently mishearing antisocial surrealism as social realism." I have replaced the term "antisocial" with "post-social," drawing from the work of Karin Knorr Cetina (2007), who writes: "Postsocial analysis assumes that social principles and structures as we have known them in the past are emptying out in Western societies, and other elements and relationships are taking their place. It assumes that new forms of binding self and other arise from the increasing role non-human objects play in a knowledge-based society and consumer culture, and from changes in the nature of objects and the structure of the self."

do. Somebody says your head isn't shaped properly so you have scientists working on the fact that it is. Somebody says you have no art, so you dredge that up. Somebody says you have no kingdoms, so you dredge that up. None of this is necessary. There will always be one more thing."

The post-social surrealists want to do something else entirely. What if, despite dehumanization—despite being reduced to fleshy machines, to organs without bodies, despite their homelands having been converted into "warren[s] for the commercial hunting of black-skins"—there were Africans who never stopped studying, learning, and (re-)creating themselves anew? What if, in the very condition designed to strip them of humanity, they discovered something profound—something that led them to question not only the terms of inclusion, but the very value of belonging to the "family of nations," and the worth of possessing anything that partakes of the character of nationality, or civil or political polity in the first place?

Ay, and what if it is this profundity they discovered that they invoke when they speak affirmatively of their Blackness and conjure otherwise worlds under the names of Afrofuturism or Afropessimism?

These post-social surrealists are not reactionaries. They are not trying to destroy civilization, no matter how deeply they may despise it, nor are they invested in saving it. They simply do not concern themselves with whether civilization persists or perishes. They make use of its means when it suits them—but they have no stake in its ends.

This book departs from the frame of social realism and moves toward the terrain of post-social surrealism. It seeks to trace and articulate something of the profundity to be found there. In doing so, it also revisits the conceptual apparatus I developed in my first four books—*Whither, Otherwise*; *Solutions for Postmodern Living*; *Improbable Aberrations and Other Idiocies*; and *Other Related Matters*. Here, that apparatus is placed in its proper context: not as an abstract formalism, but as an inheritance of, and an indebtedness to, Black post-social surrealism—what might unapologetically be called a hybrid strain of Afrofuturism and Afropessimism.

Placed in this context, much of what was hidden in the background comes to the fore. What was once withheld out of caution is now affirmed with acuity. What was lost begins, at last, to be found.

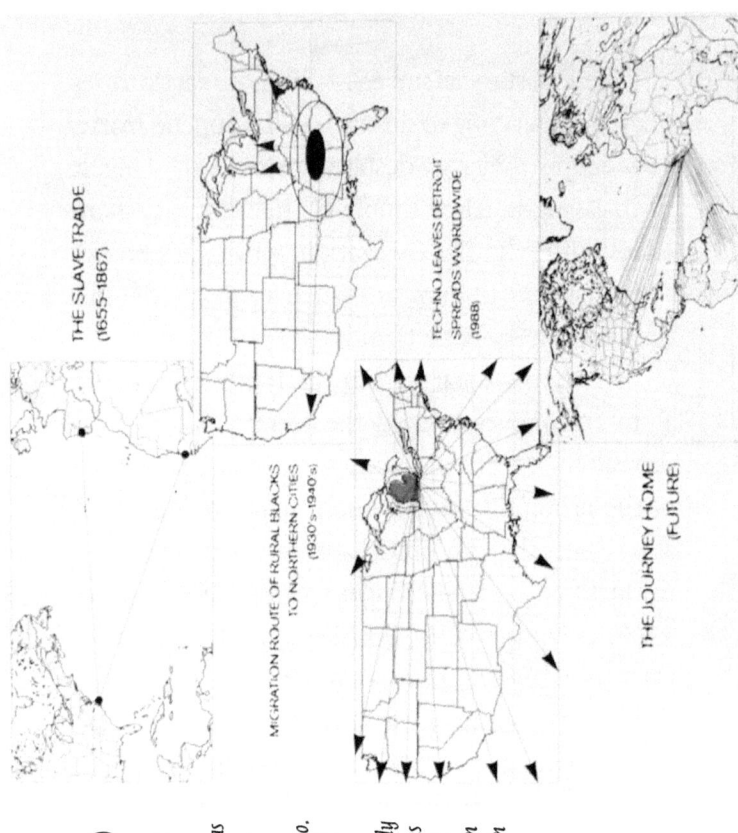

Image from the album The Quest (1997) — a Black post-social surrealist masterpiece by the Detroit Techno duo Drexciya, who pose the following inquiry:

"During the greatest holocaust the world has ever known, pregnant America-bound African slaves were thrown overboard by the thousands during labour for being sick and disruptive cargo. Is it possible that they could have given birth at sea to babies that never needed air? (...)

Are Drexciyans water breathing, aquatically mutated descendants of those unfortunate victims of human greed? Have they been spared by God to teach us or terrorise us? Did they migrate from the Gulf of Mexico to the Mississippi river basin and on to the great lakes of Michigan?

Do they walk among us? Are they more advanced than us and why do they make their strange music?

What is their Quest?"

PRELIMINARY ESSAYS

A BLACK PLANET

"Peoples who have been to the abyss do not brag of being chosen. They do not believe they are giving birth to any modern force. They live Relation and clear the way for it, to the extent that the oblivion of the abyss comes to them and that, consequently, their memory intensifies.

For though this experience made you, original victim floating toward the sea's abysses, an exception, it became something shared and made us, the descendants, one people among others. Peoples do not live on exception. Relation is not made up of things that are foreign but of shared knowledge. This experience of the abyss can now be said to be the best element of exchange."

— Édouard Glissant, from *Poetics of Relation* (1990)

During my adolescence, one of the records that deeply shaped my thinking was *Fear of a Black Planet* (1990) by Public Enemy. The music captivated me, but the title lingered in my mind even more powerfully. I felt it encapsulated something fundamental about Empire—a fear not merely of a people but of a world transformed by Blackness.

This essay redefines Blackness as a condition that both exceeds and honors ancestry. While deeply rooted in shared African descent, Blackness also extends to those whose kinship is analogical and ecological. Black cultural formations, therefore, are not solely composed of people of African descent but also include those who, under comparable pressures, develop convergent or co-evolving strategies of resistance to racial capitalism's violence. Analogical kinship arises from parallel adaptations to oppression, while ecological kinship emerges through interdependent struggles for survival. Yet, these kinships—particularly the analogical—have limits, as Black suffering remains singular in its gratuitousness. Unlike other forms of oppression, which are often rationalized within a system to serve specific functions, Black suffering is marked by its senselessness—undifferentiated, unmoored from purpose, inflicted primarily to augment others' sense of bodily integrity and the distinctiveness of their own *human* suffering. This inquiry interrogates the boundaries of solidarity, the mythologies of labor exploitation, and the ritualized violence that sustains global civil society.

Ultimately, it argues that ecological extensions of Blackness, rooted in mutual care and regeneration, offer the most viable pathway for enduring solidarities toward the planetary abolition of Empire, war, and accumulation by dispossession, degradation, and devastation.

ECOLOGICAL KINSHIP AND THE LIMITS OF ANALOGY

Homological kinship reflects shared ancestral origins, diverging over time due to differing environmental conditions and evolutionary trajectories. For instance, the bones within a whale's fins and a bat's wings—though specialized for vastly different functions—retain a common structural heritage. Life thus carries the memory of its beginnings through homology, adapting across epochs while preserving echoes of deep evolutionary inheritance. This shared foundation of ancestry informs how certain solidarities in Black cultural formations are built upon historical and genealogical ties.

Analogical kinship, however, does not arise from shared descent but from convergent adaptations. Organisms with no direct common ancestry can develop parallel traits in response to similar environmental pressures. For example, the elongated, limbless form of snakes has evolved independently across multiple reptilian lineages, offering analogous solutions to locomotion and predation. Similarly, some non-Black groups subjected to racial capitalism's techniques and technologies of power develop adaptations to oppression that mirror those of Black communities. Yet these analogies, as the essay will explore, often fall short due to the singular nature of Black suffering.

Ecological kinship, by contrast, is shaped through co-evolution and symbiotic interaction. Species evolve in mutual relationship, adapting to one another within interconnected ecosystems. The orchid *Ophrys apifera* exemplifies this dynamic, mimicking the pheromones of female bees to lure male bees as pollinators. Similarly, the elongated beaks of hummingbirds co-adapt with the tubular forms of flowers they pollinate. This deep interdependence highlights how life forms—neither homologous nor analogous—become mutually entangled through co-adaptive processes. In cultural terms, ecological kinship manifests in solidarities forged through the co-evolution of struggles, where the survival of one community is inextricably linked to the survival of another.

As noted, these categories—homological, analogical, and ecological—are not confined to biological systems but also illuminate the relational dynamics of Black solidarities. While homological kinship reflects ties rooted in shared African ancestry, Black cultural formations, like the Rainbow Coalition formed by the Black Panthers, also incorporate analogical and ecological relationships. Analogically, groups with no direct Black African ancestry in the context of modernity—such as Aboriginal Australians—have developed parallel adaptations to racial oppression, drawing inspiration from Pan-African movements and aligning with Black liberation struggles. Ecologically, Native American communities have co-evolved resistances alongside Black movements, their intertwined histories of dispossession and resilience fostering solidarities across generations. These multifaceted kinships illustrate how Black cultural formations resist the fragmenting logics of racial capitalism through both deep ancestry and adaptive interdependence.

Blackness, then, encompasses all who share a homological, analogical, or ecological relationship to the "Negro" experience. As articulated by R.A. Judy in *Sentient Flesh: Thinking in Disorder, Poiesis in Black*

(2020), this experience is shaped by the violent interpolation of racialized peoples and cosmogonies into capitalism's global order:

"[I]nterpolation into capitalism's terms of order [...] results in the dissolution of long-enduring formations of human community, engendering cosmic disorder by throwing disparate cosmogonies together under the anthropological rubric primitive. This term has a rather broad connotation, comprehending both an original inhabitant, an aboriginal, and a person belonging to a preliterate nonindustrial society, but also ancestral early man, or anything else that is archaic. It has been inclusively applied to a wide array of types of natives—also a conceptual category—engendered along the way in capitalism's global expansion and colonial rule. Not all colonial natives are designated primitive, however; there are those who belong to age-old civilizations, the effects of which, according to the narrative of translatio, transferred westward to feed the foundations of capitalism—outstanding examples of which are China, India, and most of the Muslim world. The distinction of having been civilizationally long-in-the-tooth does not mitigate the disordering effects of capitalist expansion, however. On the contrary, being construed as archaic civilizational formations surpassed by Western capitalist modernity is another sense of primitive and tends to exacerbate the disordering effects with an aura of civilizational degradation and loss of authenticity. Terminologically, primitive and Negro share the same semantic space to the point of synonymy. Those populations designated Negro, however, are seemingly always primitive, this attributed state playing a role, almost as a neo-Aristotelian afterthought, in legitimating their designation: the absurdly Hegelian argument that the primitive, enslaved and made Negro, enters into civilization and thus benefits from the transformation."

Through this expansive framework, we see that Blackness is not merely a matter of racial categorization but a condition produced by, and resistant to, the violent impositions of Western capitalist modernity's project of "civilization." It forms solidarities across homological, analogical, and ecological lines, countering the reductionist logics that have long fragmented human relationality and planetary life under colonial terms of order.

Yet, in expanding the definition of Blackness here, it is important to note that Black politics does exclude some. Those who lack or repudiate a Black ancestry that would form homological kinship and simultaneously disavow the parallel and co-evolving resistance to racial capitalism that defines both analogical and ecological kinships cannot be subsumed under Blackness. This boundary is crucial to preserving the integrity of Black cultural formations and their historically specific modes of resistance and survival.

That being said, it is possible for those excluded from Blackness to "become-Black" through suffering racial capitalist oppression and either being compelled to adopt analogous forms of resistance or, alternatively, endeavoring to co-evolve their resistance to racial capitalism alongside Black people

This process of becoming-Black, particularly through ecological kinship, can be likened to the symbiotic relationship between the orchid and its pollinating wasp. Just as the wasp enables the orchid's survival by spreading its pollen, those who engage in solidarity with Black struggles contribute to the flourishing of Black resistance. This mutual adaptation, grounded in reciprocal nourishment, allows diverse communities to thrive in interdependence, nurturing a world where resistance, like a resilient ecosystem, is continuously regenerated through acts of shared care and struggle.

It is important to contrast becoming-Black by way of ecological kinship with becoming-Black through analogical kinship, because the latter is fraught with limitations. As *Afropessimism* teaches, Black suffering is singular in its abjection, such that no form of oppression experienced by others is truly analogous to the gratuitous violence inflicted on Black people. As Frank Wilderson III (2020) explains, the ritualized display of Black death and dismemberment functions as a perverse form of healing for (post-)modern global racial capitalist civil society—soothing its anxieties through spectacles that violate the integrity of Black bodies, reducing them to flesh, organs without bodies.

"Civil society does not want Black land as it wants Indian land, that it might distinguish the Nation from Turtle Island; it does not want Black consent, as it wants working-class consent, that it might distinguish a capitalist economic system from a socialist one, that it might extract surplus value and turn that value into profit. What civil society needs from Black people is far more essential, far more fundamental than land and profits. What civil society needs from Black people is confirmation of Human existence."

[...]

"Blacks are not going to be genocided like Native Americans. We are being genocided, but genocided and regenerated, because the spectacle of Black death is essential to the mental health of the world—we can't be wiped out completely, because our deaths must be repeated, visually. The bodily mutilation of Blackness is necessary, so it must be repeated."

Wilderson emphasizes that such violence functions as a ritual that stabilizes the anxieties of non-Black people, offering a grotesque form of reassurance:

"What we are witnessing on YouTube, Instagram, and the nightly news as murders are rituals of healing for civil society. Rituals that stabilize and ease the anxiety that other people feel in their daily lives. I know I am a Human because I am not Black. I know I am not Black because when and if I experience the kind of violence Blacks experience, there is a reason, some contingent transgression."

The singularity of Blackness lies in the fact that Black people are reproduced to be enslaved, tortured, dismembered, and murdered—by commission and omission—without reason and distinction, a condition that affirms the sense and distinctiveness of the bodily integrity and humanity of those who are not Black. Others die for a reason, be it a good reason or a bad one; Black people die so that others might recognize the distinction between dying for a reason and dying for no reason at all. Others fear being brutalized, imprisoned, or murdered for one reason or another, good or bad; Black people fear being brutalized, imprisoned, or murdered for no reason at all. Others fear that care and support may be denied to them for justifiable or unjustifiable reasons; Black people fear that there is no reason, justifiable or unjustifiable, for others to care or support them at all.

The popular myth that African people were enslaved purely or primarily for free labor collapses under the weight of the gratuitous violence inflicted on the enslaved. As Karl Marx described, Africa was converted into "a warren for the commercial hunting of black-skins," but the tortures inflicted upon these black-skins reveal that this was not merely a matter of labor exploitation—it was a spectacle of senseless, inhumane brutality that stood in stark contrast to the non-Black, non-slave's sense of human distinction and bodily integrity. In *Lose Your Mother* (2006), Saidiya Hartman obliterates this myth by recounting only a few of the tortures endured by enslaved Africans across the globe—acts perpetrated at the very same time that the humanism born of the Renaissance and the Enlightenment was consolidating itself.

"In the Gold Coast, his ears were cut off and then he was put to death. In São Tomé, he was drowned in the sea. In Dahomey, he was decapitated. In Kongo, he was asphyxiated in a barracoon.

In Santo Domingo, boiling sugarcane was poured on his head and withered the flesh on his body. In Barbados, he was flogged with a seven-headed whip. In Cuba, he was filled with gunpowder and blown up with a match. In St. John, he was burned at the stake, sawed in half, and impaled. In Maryland, he was hanged and decapitated. In Georgia, he was covered with sugar and buried in an anthill. In Curaçao, his face was scorched and his head cut off and placed on a pole for the amusement of vultures. In Surinam, they cut off his hands and crushed his head with a sledgehammer. In Trinidad, he was dismembered and his body parts were thrown into the Atlantic. In Brazil, his ears were chopped off and a dagger buried in his back, his putrefied head displayed in the central square. In Panama, a sword disemboweled him. In Lima, he was paraded through the streets, beaten with the lash, and his wounds were washed with urine and rum. In Jamaica, he was force-fed excrement and burned on a pyre. In Grenada, he was shoved into a kiln and roasted. In Paramaribo, they cut his Achilles tendon and amputated his right leg. In Virginia, he was skinned. In Texas, his feet were bound and he was dragged through the streets by a horse. In New York, he was beaten with cudgels and hanged from a lamppost. In North Carolina, they burned him with torches and threw his body into quicklime. In Mississippi, he was cut to pieces on a wheel of blades. In Washington, D.C., he was mounted like a beast of burden and driven to death. In Alabama, he was tied to a cross, scourged by flaming torches, and beaten with chains. In Louisiana, his belly was sliced open and his entrails spilled out."

The reality of the Black condition is so horrific that it overwhelms the psyche, leading many Black people to disavow it and embrace myths. Hoping to escape the condition of being "just another mass of Black flesh," some construct spurious reasons to explain the inexplicable: they invent and then refute justifications for what was never meant to be justified. Those who succeed most convincingly in this endeavor—who persuade the world that their lives and deaths have "meaning"—become Black persons of distinction, "special cases," granted the "privilege" of having a reason either to live life to term or to suffer premature death, becoming exceptions within the broader framework of gratuitous violence.

The general suffering of other groups under racial capitalism may resemble that of Black people in manner but not in meaning. Indeed, the fact that their suffering typically holds meaning—serves a purpose or explanation within the system—sets a clear limit to the analogy. Only in special cases is the brutalization, imprisonment, or murder of non-Black people under racial capitalism transformed into a gratuitous and meaningless spectacle. Black suffering, by contrast, is typically gratuitous, devoid of inherent meaning—except in such "special cases." It is only through these exceptional figures that analogies between Black and non-Black suffering find their strongest, though still limited, basis.

For this reason, the planetary extension of Blackness ecologically is the only viable extension. Analogical extensions of Blackness may hold some value, but only insofar as they create the conditions for genuine ecological kinship—where solidarity becomes a shared process of mutual survival and regeneration, rooted in a recognition of interdependence rather than the illusion of equivalence. A Black planet, in this sense, represents a planetary resistance to projects of "civilization" arising from Western capitalist modernity—a resistance defined by the ecological extension of Blackness across the Earth. This planetary resistance does not erase or subsume the singularity of Black suffering; instead, it honors that singularity as the foundational condition that both anchors and informs all solidarities. Resistance to Empire, therefore, does not require the flattening of differences but the cultivation of a web of co-evolutionary struggles, where the recognition of gratuitous violence and shared care coalesce into a regenerative force. In this vision, a Black planet is not only a refusal of racial capitalism's terms of order but a horizon of collective liberation where human and more-than-human life can thrive.

A LESSON IN THE BLACK ARTS & DECOLONIAL SCIENCES

The following is the text of a lecture delivered on 24 May 2025 to open the workshop Futurhythmachines: Infopoeisis, *presented as part of the exhibition* How to See in the Dark, *organized by the Center for Concrete and Abstract Machines.*

I begin with Aimé Césaire's *Discourse on Colonialism* (1950):

"I am talking about societies drained of their essence, cultures trampled underfoot, institutions undermined, lands confiscated, religions smashed, magnificent artistic creations destroyed, extraordinary possibilities wiped out. [...] The Indians massacred, the Moslem world drained of itself, the Chinese world defiled and perverted for a good century; the Negro world disqualified; mighty voices stilled forever; homes scattered to the wind; all this wreckage, all this waste, humanity reduced to a monologue, and you think all that does not have its price?"

Césaire's words anchor my inquiry: What has all this devastation cost science?

I call the forms of knowledge resulting from this devastation Colonial Science—forms entangled with imperial domination, extraction, and epistemic violence. This is a science complicit in genocides, ethnocides, and ecocides, bound to the horrors Césaire describes. Yet, other sciences exist—Decolonial Sciences—knowledges produced by and for colonized peoples in both defiance of and divergence from Empire's machinery of brutalization.

The "brute matter" and "brute facts" of Colonial Science are not givens: they are made by Colonial Science through processes of brutalization. Colonizers submit beings to scientific study not out of curiosity but with the intent to brutalize—to make efficient use of force, disintegrate, break down into bits, and transform subjects into perversely pleasurable and profitable datum for collection, correction, consumption, and deletion.

It is only when beings resist brutalization in remarkable ways that Colonial Science calls in its specialists in complexity, chaos, indeterminacy, and noise—its reinforcements for risk management and damage control. At this stage, Colonial Science endeavors to marginalize those beings remarkable for resisting brutalization, reducing them to special cases, subjects for specialized knowledge, and thus rendering them inaccessible to the global majority.

Decolonial Sciences, however, are committed to: (i) deconstructing the colonial practices of brutalization and specialization entrenched in the colonial techno-scientific imagination; and (ii) (re-)constructing "other-whys" that enable knowledge producers and wisdom keepers to approach beings otherwise than through brutalization and specialization.

Given my background and musical sensibilities, I am particularly drawn to the Decolonial Sciences of African and Afro-diasporic peoples, especially their radical experiments with sound. As Dhanveer Singh Brar (2021), drawing on Paul Gilroy's *The Black Atlantic* (1993), explains:

"Historically, [Black] slaves were refused access to written language and textual mechanics as part of the racial codification of the modern subject. Thus [...] the phonic and the aural became the engines for communicative and performative practice amongst the enslaved. [...] [S]uch a maneuver had two effects: one, the seemingly senseless noise-making of the slaves only confirmed the perception of their pre-modernity on the part of those who traded and owned them; two, such presumptions allowed New World blacks to nuance and experiment with the sonic as a field of expression with only relatively minor interference. Such partial autonomy was crucial [...] because it allowed black diasporans to develop a socially inflected sonic technology known as 'antiphony (call and response).'"

Brar reveals how colonial dismissal of Black sound as "senseless noise" inadvertently created a fugitive space where sound became a site of experimental knowledge—relational, adaptive, and deeply philosophical.

Yet, the history of the African diaspora is too often framed as one of rupture, as if the violence of the transatlantic slave trade severed African peoples from their cultural roots entirely. A more fitting metaphor is diffraction: a bending and scattering that transforms rather than destroys. The Door of No Return and the Middle Passage were not points of total severance but apertures through which African cosmologies were diffracted into new forms—warped, yet enduring.

The forced displacement of African peoples did not erase cultural continuities but revealed their transformative potential. Polyrhythms, call-and-response structures, possession rituals, and ubuntu-rooted communal practices traversed the Middle Passage not as broken fragments but as dynamic forces. Adapting to and through the Indigenous and European worldviews they encountered, these forces generated hybrid spiritual and sonic technologies capable of resisting and persisting despite profound violence.

To borrow a phrase from Amiri Baraka, the "changing same" of Afro-diasporic traditions reveals diffraction as a generative process—continuity not as rupture, but as expansion and transformation. Yoruba Egungun masquerades, which honor the ancestral dead, find echoes in Haitian Vodou's Gede spirits—irreverent figures who mend the breach between life and death through humor and ritual. The Kongo cosmogram, a sacred map of the crossroads as a site of spiritual convergence, (re-)encounters and (re-)combines with the Yoruba orisha of the crossroads, Eshu, to be transfigured into Haitian Vodou's Papa Legba and his veve cosmogram. The divinatory wisdom of Ifá, carried by enslaved Yoruba, transformed into Santería's and Candomblé's cowrie shell readings—each adapting to new geographies while retaining core structures for producing relationality, revelation, and transformation.

These lineages reveal that the sonic and spiritual

technologies of the Niger-Congo continuum—a linguistic, rhythmic, and psychic field that traversed the African continent—flowed through the Door of No Return and endured the Middle Passage not as shattered fragments but as diffracted/diffracting waves, scattering while amplifying their generative force.

Returning to the core of my inquiry, I propose that the Black Arts—and Black music in particular—have long served as modes and expressions of Decolonial Science. These sonic technologies, deeply philosophical and profoundly relational, have often been disqualified from the category of "science" precisely because they had to cloak themselves in what colonial authority dismissed as "senseless noise." Yet beneath this misreading lies a vast reservoir of experimental knowledge—one that continues to resist, adapt, and transform under colonial violence.

What I am offering you today will do little for those bound to the frameworks of Colonial Science. But it may speak powerfully to those seeking to break free from the logics of colonial domination and produce a Decolonial Science—an epistemic praxis in apposition and opposition to Empire.

Indeed, those still beholden to the frameworks of Colonial Science may struggle to recognize what

I present here as "science" at all. For the refusal to acknowledge the profound depths of African and Afro-diasporic knowledge systems—their philosophy, methodology, and radical relationality—remains part of the price science continues to pay for Empire's disqualification of the Negro world.

THE POWERS SHAPING BLACK MUSIC

"Music, as paradoxical as it might seem, is the result of thought. It is the result of thought perfected at its most empirical, i.e., as attitude or stance."

—Amiri Baraka, Blues People (1963)

Black music is not merely expressive. It is experimental. It is a Decolonial Science, practiced against the grain of anti-Black violence—at once a life-support system, a diagnostic instrument, and a carrier of resistance. Across centuries, it has metabolized Empire's evolving machineries of domination to yield forms that defy capture, refuse erasure, and amplify the irreducible complexity of Black beings and becomings.

Black music does not arise outside of power, but through and against its operations. From the earliest colonial contact to the algorithmic present,

Black sound has moved in fugitive counterpoint to four evolving modalities of domination: ruling, disciplinary, normalizing, and optimizing power. These powers did not emerge all at once. They arrived in historical sequence—layered like sediment, folding, fracturing, compacting, and metamorphosing under the ongoing pressure of Black insistence, persistence, and resistance. Each mode of power reconfigures the terrain of domination, adapting to resistance by inventing new techniques of control.

The narrative that follows centers the trajectory of Black music—from Blues to Techno—in the United States, not only for its internal richness, but for its broad dissemination across the Pan-African continuum—a diffusion shaped in no small part by U.S. global hegemony and the export of America's particularly virulent strains of anti-Blackness. Yet this music is part of a much larger diffraction. Parallel sonic lineages have unfolded throughout the Afro-diasporic world: from Samba to Funk Carioca in Brazil, from Marabi to Gqom in South Africa, from Swahili Taarab to Singeli in Dar es Salaam, from Calypso in the Caribbean to Jungle in the UK. Each genre emerged in response to specific regimes of domination and in creative defiance of them—carrying forward a shared insistence on life, complexity, and (re-)creation under constraint. These forms did not evolve in isolation; they reverberate across the Black world through material circuits of mutual influence, embodied memory, and sonic experimentation.

The pre-modern world saw the emergence of ruling and disciplinary powers as the primary mechanisms of anti-Blackness. Iberian Catholic enslavers—plagiarizing the racial logics of Islamic Arab slave systems—cast Blackness as a spiritual defect to be subdued. This was not yet the biological "race" of modernity, but Blackness was already marked as disposable, deviant, and subordinated. Ruling power operated through ritualized spectacle—public tortures and executions, legal decrees, religious inquisitions—staged to assert white supremacy and sanctify domination. Disciplinary power, in turn, governed the enslaved body through routine examinations, forced labor, catechism, and surveillance, rendering Black life measurable and correctable within a violently imposed order.

These pre-modern modalities of power, however, were largely localized. They targeted those caught directly within Empire's rituals of domination—those enslaved, examined, indoctrinated. But with modernity's technocratic turn, new formations came into their own: normalizing power and optimizing power. The former generalized anti-Blackness to encompass all Black life, while the latter engineered exceptions—optimizing select individuals as its proxies within an adaptive and self-regulating system.

Normalizing power objectified anti-Black myths and stereotypes, transmuting them into technical data and statistical "facts." Through biased metrics, aggregated data, and taxonomic patterning, it recast Blackness as inherently pathological—regardless of legal status. With the rise of social science and the apparatus of population management, Black life was no longer merely captured—it was counted, abstracted, predicted, and controlled. Under normalization, even the freed became suspect. Subjugation no longer hinged on enslavement alone; all Black life, regardless of class, proximity to power, or aspiration, was rendered subordinate.

Normalizing powers came into their own in and through the transition from enslavement to emancipation. And it is precisely from this terrain of post-emancipation containment that Blues emerges—not as an aesthetic seeking recognition, but as a fugitive epistemology. A lyrical science of refusal. Blues speaks from the underside of emancipation, where freedom existed in law but criminalization prevailed in practice. It does not aspire to universalism—it bears witness to what normalization renders invisible: the moan, the stomp, the sideways joke. It is intimate, partisan, and unquantifiable. Blues marks the emergence of a new sonic methodology—one that rejects data, defies statistics, and insists on the sovereignty of felt experience.

From that moan, Soul emerges—not as a rupture, but as a diffraction. It softens the raw edges of Blues into a harmonic bridge between the grief of the dispossessed and the aspirations of a Black middle class striving to "make it" in an anti-Black world. Soul retains the spirit of struggle while daring to imagine reconciliation. In an era when normalization offered tentative inclusion through policy and performance, it became the soundtrack of belief—not in the legitimacy of Empire, but in the possibility that Black life might transform it from within. It reached for kinship amid volatility, holding both faith and fatigue.

But hope under Empire was always provisional—and eventually confronted its limits. As normalizing power gave way to the ascendance of optimizing power, the lie of inclusion became harder to sustain. Optimization reframed domination as individual deficiency, selling productivity, personal branding, and self-regulation as the new currencies of liberation. It trained the body to perform merit while obscuring the architecture of structural exclusion. Just as this regime began to prevail, Funk emerged—not to soothe, but to interrupt. It ground against the gears of optimization. It grooved against the grain of manufactured hope. Funk named what optimization worked to conceal: that no amount of hustle could outrun Empire's metrics. It didn't theorize the lie— it broke it down. Syncopated, irreverent, and defiantly alive.

Hip-Hop emerged from the rubble of optimization's broken promises. Redlined, incarcerated, digitized, and policed, Black communities forged in Hip-Hop a new method—sampling the ruins, remixing memory, and using bits to make breaks. Its poetic verses scripted escape routes from the myth of the "talented tenth." It named these figures for what they were: optimized proxies, emissaries of Empire cloaked in excellence. And Hip-Hop called them out—with poetic measures of street cred that outweighed the technocratic metrics of academic and professional success.

Not all refusal involves the verbal or lyric. Some lives in abstraction, in dissonance, in the refusal to be contained. Jazz, a contemporary of Blues, confronted normalization not through narration but through deviation. It scrambled the metric grid, fractured harmony, and played outside. Like cosmograms and divinatory mantics that crossed the Middle Passage, Jazz became a ritual technology—a sonic practice of entanglement, tension, and improvisation. It held contradiction in suspension. It did not explain—it enacted.

As optimization deepened—disciplining through dashboards, coaching through algorithms, isolating through performance metrics—Black sonic resistance mutated once more. House and Techno, close siblings born of queer Black dance floors in Chicago and the post-industrial ruins of Detroit, were not lyrical forms. They did not name the wound—they varied its frequencies. Built from pulses, loops, and polyrhythms, they composed trance architectures that rewired the nervous system—not for performance, but for release. These were not genres of legibility, but of saturation. They bypassed the logic of optimization and retrained the body not for productivity, but for attunement to the tidalectics of presence and absence, noise and silence.

In these spaces, Blackness was not represented—it was resonated. Not translated, but transmitted—through rhythm, saturation, and relation. House and Techno became machinic rituals, repurposing instruments of capture into engines of communion. Where optimization demanded conformity and control, they offered queerness and release.

But the story does not end with production. Domination also governs consumption. The very systems that give rise to Black music expose it to distortion, displacement, and extraction. Yet not all forms yield equally. Blues and Hip-Hop, grounded in vernacular specificity and testimonial force, resist seamless appropriation. Their power resides in their rootedness—in a world. To imitate them without that world is to echo a hollow sound, and so they are exaggerated, stylized, and staged by the culture industry to make that world visible, legible—available for surveillance and spectacle.

Jazz, House, and Techno, more abstract and less visibly tethered to Blackness, can be misread and misrepresented as neutral or universal. Their refusal of Empire's legibility—the very source of their subversive force—makes them vulnerable to Empire's extractive embrace. When white musicians mine these forms to embellish their own sensibilities or refine the Western canon, they risk enacting the logic of optimization—assimilating, exoticizing, or instrumentalizing difference to reinforce the dominant core.

And yet, not all white relation to Black sound is extraction. Some approach Black music not as resource, but as method—a praxis of unlearning, a disruption of whiteness itself. These uncommon—or better, undercommon—gestures carry an ethical orientation: not mastery, but transformation. Still, even these efforts remain peripheral to the heart of the thing, which continues to pulse elsewhere—in the sonic laboratories forged under duress, where survival meets speculation, and sound becomes a strategy for living otherwise.

Because Black Jazz and Black Techno—unlike their white mimics—are not deviations or derivations, but continuations. They extend experiments that precede, exceed, and succeed them. They remember. They recreate. They do not aestheticize struggle—they work it, remix it, riff on it, and move with and through it.

As creative forms of resistance to the machinery of Empire—countering ruling, disciplinary, normalizing, and optimizing powers—Black music is not merely reactive. It is experimental. Diagnostic. World-making. It teaches us to listen otherwise: to hear the break in the beat, the grain against which we groove, the world that turns and returns within the loop. And because all four powers persist, all Black musics persist in opposition. Blues, Jazz, Soul, Funk, Hip-Hop, House, Techno—these are not discrete genres progressing in linear succession, but confluent streams that wind, merge, and diverge—overlapping currents within a broader sonic watershed. They improvise collectively, and in relation to other so-called "genres" across the Pan-African continuum—Samba, Cumbia, Rumba, Highlife, Calypso, Reggae, Merengue, Zouk, Dancehall, Jungle—to counter domination and compose alternative modes of being.

In this sense, they constitute a decolonial praxis—what composer Anthony Braxton calls *Trans-African Functionalism*: a collective strategy of sound, survival, and speculative construction. A practice that does not merely reflect the world, but alters its coordinates.

And yet, even as Black music functions as a site of resistance and world-making, it is not immune to cooptation from within. There are Black creators who, knowingly or not, produce music for consumption by white audiences—works designed to satisfy the gaze and palate of Empire. In such cases, what Braxton terms "Black Exotica" emerges: a sonic performance of difference calibrated not to disrupt white desire, but to entertain or affirm it. This, too, is part of the landscape—another signal shaped by domination's demand.

To hear clearly, then, is not only to identify resistance—but to counter its counterfeits. To attune ourselves not only to rhythm, but to relation. Not only to the sound, but to its direction.

Epistemics of the Black Radical Tradition: Break Beats, Blue Notes, Ring Shouts

The paradigmatic sonic inventions of African and Afro-diasporic knowledge systems are three: break beats, blue notes, and ring shouts. To understand these paradigmatic inventions, one must develop a sense of rhythm, both metrical and spectral.

A *metrical rhythm* consists of pulses slow enough to be perceived as a sequence of discrete pulsations or beats—time articulated through countable moments.

A *spectral rhythm* consists of pulses so rapid they blur into a continuous vibration, perceived simultaneously as pitch and timbre, sustained over varying durations.

Polyrhythm emerges when multiple rhythms co-exist, generating tension between concurrent patterns.

Metrical polyrhythm layers multiple discrete pulsations or beats, each articulated according to a distinct meter.

Spectral polyrhythm layers multiple continuous vibrations, each articulated according to a distinct frequency.

In *African Rhythm and African Sensibility: Aesthetics and Social Action in African Musical Idioms* (1981), John Miller Chernoff makes the following observations about metrical polyrhythm:

If the rhythmic systems used by different African people are not the same (though they are often surprisingly similar), they at least have in common the fact that they are complex. [...] In African music, there are always at least two rhythms going on. Musicologists call this polymeter or multiple meter, the simultaneous use of different meters. African music cannot be notated without assigning different meters to the different instruments in an ensemble.

The effect of polymetric music is as if different rhythms were competing for our attention. No sooner do we grasp one rhythm than we lose track of it and hear another. Each musician contributes their own part in a total polymetric fabric.

Yet Chernoff, despite this profound insight, repeatedly underemphasizes half of his own observation. Throughout the book, he describes African music as "music-to-find-the-beat-by," while neglecting the equally vital dimension: losing the beat. The essence of African rhythm lies in the generative tension between losing and finding the beat. To borrow his own language, African music is as much "music-to-lose-the-beat-to" as it is "music-to-find-the-beat-by." Indeed, it is the *break beat*—the cross beat that encourages and enables us to lose one beat and, at the same moment, find another—that constitutes the music's most characteristic feature. African music, then, might be more accurately described as music-to-break-to, a break being by turns (i) the breakdown of a beat-being-lost and (ii) the breakthrough of a beat-being-found.

This framework clarifies Chernoff's next claim:

The fundamental characteristic of African music is the way the music works with time in the dynamic clash and interplay of cross rhythms. There is always more than one "time" in the music. In Western music and Western science, "time" is treated as a single, objective phenomenon, moving in steady intervals towards some distant moment. Western music is about ordering sound through time, imposing a strict order on time. In contrast, in the African context, both the musician and the spectator maintain an additional rhythm (an additional time) to give coherence to the ensemble. The essential point is the need to mediate the rhythms actively. In the Western context, when several tones are heard together, they are taken as a unity, and the term harmony or chord expresses the oneness of the sound. In African music, there are different beats and variations that fit within the beat; and one participates in the music by integrating various rhythms to perceive the beat. The beat arises from the whole relationship of the rhythms rather than from any particular part. The most relevant feature of African music is that the way rhythms are established in relationship creates a tension in time. African music depends on the resistance of the parts to fuse. The music is engaging because the tension must be comprehended without undermining the power and vitality that comes from conflict between different rhythms.

Even in this otherwise brilliant passage, Chernoff's assertion that "African music depends on the resistance of the parts to fuse" might be more accurately reframed: African music depends on the insistence and persistence of the break.

What the break beat represents for metrical rhythms in African music, the *blue note* represents for spectral rhythms. Just as one can speak of losing and finding the beat in metrical polyrhythm, one can speak of losing and finding the note in spectral polyrhythm.

To understand what is at stake here, it is important to recognize that spectral rhythm accounts not only for pitch but also for timbre—the unique texture of sound created by variations in how a note vibrates. Two instruments, like a trumpet and a violin, intoning the same pitch will sound different because their harmonic overtones—those subtle, overlapping frequencies—oscillate in unique patterns. Likewise, a single instrument, like a piano, intoning the same pitch but with a different attack—a hammer blow versus a light touch—will sound different because the style of the attack alters the harmonic overtones.

In addition to the previously examined propensity for multiple meter, a critical feature of African music is the ubiquity of a percussive performance style and the importance of the manner in which a player attacks their instrument. Whereas in Western tonal frameworks, the most desirable attack tends to land directly on its intended pitch, in African musics, the most desirable attack often percussively lands elsewhere before winding up at its intended pitch and wavering around it.

This percussive landing, winding up, and wavering produces a spectral polyrhythm akin to the metrical polyrhythms that characterize African musics: overlapping spectral rhythms that do not fuse into orderly harmonic alignment but, rather, continually drift out of strict harmonic synchrony. This attack pattern is experienced by the listener as a blue note: a harmonic drift, a losing and finding of a note, that betrays a spectral polyrhythmicity.

Given the break beat and the blue note, some might say that African musicians play around the beat or off-beat, and that they play around the note or off-key. This, however, is inaccurate, for it is the ability to identify the on-beat and on-key note that enables the listener to engage with the music fully. Musicians play in such a way that finding the on-beat and on-key note becomes both a sensual and intellectual challenge for the listener.

To experience African music, one must be able to hold in mind an additional beat and note beyond what is heard. Whenever the player moves off-beat or off-key, breaking the beat or drifting into the blue, they do so in a way that calls the listener to respond on-beat and on-key.

This dynamic tension distinguishes the antiphonies of African music from those in Western traditions. The call-and-response invites not passive following but active participation, transforming the listener into a sense-maker—dancing, clapping, and singing along on-beat and on-key in response to calls that break off-beat and drift off-key in to the blue. In other words, the players position themselves as accompaniment, generating off-beat and off-key conditions for the listeners to take the lead in sense-making.

More profoundly still, as the listener takes the lead and loses themself in sense-making, they tend to find themselves charged with taking on the role of accompaniment—dancing, clapping, and singing off-beat (break beats) and off-key (blue notes) so as to invite others into the space of sense-making alongside them. Just as the break beat and blue note create tension through losing and finding rhythm and pitch, so too do the roles of player and listener, caller and responder, continuously dissolve and emerge within the confluence of participatory antiphony. The responder loses themself as responder, becoming the caller, while the caller loses themself as caller, becoming the responder.

Synecdochically, we will refer to such practices of improvisatory and participatory antiphony, call-and-response, as *"ring shouts"*—the ring shout being an exemplary form of this practice. Originating in African diasporic spiritual practices, the ring shout involves a communal, polyrhythmic dance where participants move counterclockwise in a circle, singing, clapping, and stomping while responding to a lead caller. The shifting roles of caller and responder, dancer and accompanist, make the ring shout a living embodiment of collective sense-making through rhythm and voice.

Western(ized) consumers who primarily encounter African and Afro-diasporic musical products in the processed and commodified forms preferred by the culture industry—extracted from the communities and contexts that informed their emergence—may hear the break beats and blue notes but fail to recognize them as calls, invitations for antiphonal participation that transform passive listening into a collective practice of sense-making. They remain consumers.

Western(ized) academics, who similarly encounter African and Afro-diasporic musical products in these degraded forms or, when not that, engage them as distant observers and theorists—whether as anthropologists, ethnographers, sociologists, or other humanities researchers—often fail to recognize these calls for antiphonal participation. And when they do recognize the calls, they too often fail to respond to them, choosing instead to "observe" and "theorize" rather than participate and invite others to participate.

Yet break beats, blue notes, and ring shouts are neither mere phonographic material for commodification and consumption nor ethnographic material for observation and theorization. They are paradigmatic vehicles for the dissemination and experimentation of a Decolonial Science.

Here, my aim is not merely to theorize this Decolonial Science but to practice it with you—by involving you directly in the making of what the authorities of Colonial Science are bound to dismiss as "senseless noise."

Futurhythmachines: From Data Collection and Analysis to Signal Sampling & Synthesis

Colonial Science brutalizes us into bits of data to be collected and analyzed, seeking to rationally represent phenomena by reducing our complexity to visual and symbolic abstractions.

By contrast, drawing upon the (re-)creative methodologies of Black electronic dance musics, we will experiment with decolonial practices of signal sampling and synthesis—methodologies that run counter to colonial practices of data extraction and analysis. Our aim is not to represent phenomena through reductive models but to intuitively sense phenomena that elude representational and analytical frameworks. Using the layered polyrhythms and participatory antiphonies characteristic of Black electronic dance musics, the practices of sampling and synthesis we will explore here engage with phenomena dynamically, attuning to their resonances and relational patterns.

Turning to Gilbert Simondon's processual and synthetic notion of information—and away from Claude Shannon's rational and analytic paradigm—this project in decolonial science proposes a shift in how we engage with data. Where Shannon's model fixates on the transmission of discrete bits, Simondon emphasizes the dynamic emergence of form and meaning through relational fields of resonance. This shift is inspired by the ways Black electronic dance musics transform sonic fragments into dynamic, processual soundscapes that resist rigid abstraction while embracing confluence and improvisation.

Rather than extracting discrete bits for representation, we will emphasize tuning into the rhythms and flows of events to discern patterns and possibilities obscured by conventional analysis. Through a deconstruction of prevailing methods for representing the past and present as numerical abstractions, we will undertake experiments resonant with the ethos of Black electronic dance musics, which take decontextualized histories and disparate sounds and (de/re)compose them into communal and immersive sonic experiences.

We will explore the break beats, blue notes, and ring shouts that drive collective sense-making among emcees, deejays, selectors, and dancers—not simply as aesthetic practices but as epistemic ones. Like these sonic forms, our inquiry will resist linear projections and causal chains, embracing instead rhythmic and resonant gestures as pathways for sense-making and the co-creation of emergent futures.

Break beats, blue notes, and ring shouts—the paradigmatic inventions of Afro-diasporic rhythmanalysts—are "abstract futurhythmachines." The synthesizers and samplers with which Afro-diasporic rhythmanalysts generate break beats, blue notes, and ring shouts are "concrete futurhythmachines." In theory, our focus here will be on the abstract rather than the concrete; in practice, however, we must tend to the concrete in order to articulate the abstract. Thus, we will be experimenting with samplers and synthesizers to generate break beats, blue notes, and ring shouts.

On Anexactitude in Decolonial Science: From Error to Errantry

The shift from data collection and analysis to sampling and synthesis signals a profound epistemic transformation: a movement from error to errantry. Caribbean poet and philosopher Édouard Glissant, in *Poetics of Relation* (1990), describes errantry as a radical departure from totalizing systems of knowledge, emphasizing relationality, multiplicity, and the refusal of closure. This shift challenges the colonial fixation on control, mastery, and the reduction of complexity into extractable "truth."

Colonial science is anchored in the dichotomy of "random error" (noise) and "systematic error" (bias). It presumes a stable, measurable reality where knowledge production depends on minimizing noise while biasing outcomes toward desired results. Consider the social scientist addressing recidivism rates: rather than asking what relational conditions produce cycles of incarceration, the question becomes how to intervene to bias reality toward lower recidivism. The world is framed as a field of variables to adjust, with success measured by the elimination of noise—the entanglements that disrupt clean causal claims. Bias is reduced to a technical flaw rather than a structuring principle of colonial knowledge itself.

This mode of experimentation is monometric: it imposes a single, synchronized measure of time and order where all variables align to a predetermined rhythm of control. It is symphonic, seeking harmonic unity under a dominant key, where discordance is corrected. And it is orchestrated, with knowledge production centralized under the authority of a composer-conductor, figures who define both the scope and limits of inquiry. The colonial scientist directs from above, seeking outcomes aligned with systems of power and capital.

Errantry unsettles this order. While colonial science is monometric, decolonial science is polymetric. Where colonial science is symphonic, decolonial science is polyphonic. Where colonial science is orchestrated, decolonial science is improvised—unfolding in confluence with the world, not as its master but as a participant in its infinite rhythms and relations.

The Break Beat: Polymetrics & the Generativity of Dissensus

The break beat, central to Afro-diasporic musical traditions, challenges the monometric by embodying polymetricity—multiple, independent meters coexisting in tension without being subordinated to a single measure. John Miller Chernoff observes that African music "cannot be notated without assigning different measures to the different instruments in an ensemble." This irreducible multiplicity generates vitality through rhythmic tension, not resolution.

The break beat's power lies in its refusal of unifying standard measures. Each rhythm maintains its own measure in dynamic relationship with the others. The propulsiveness of the music emerges not from resolution but from the tension between overlapping measures, as listeners and players lose and find the beat across shifting temporalities. The break beat, a transversal that cuts across multiple measures, amplifies difference—it does not disrupt but articulates their entanglements.

Colonial science, by contrast, imposes a monometric logic. All variables must be synchronized to a unified/universal standard. Its goal is epistemic consensus, enforcing a single framework of intelligibility. Rhythmic tension—like epistemic variability—is treated as error, a failure to achieve coherence. Colonial science disciplines knowledge into alignment, endeavoring to resolve dissensus into consensus.

Decolonial science, through the paradigmatic vehicle of the break beat, refuses this flattening of difference. It honors the coexistence of multiple epistemic measures without collapsing them into a single overarching one. Knowledge here arises not from enforced order but from the generative tension between measures. To practice decolonial science is to remain present with this dissensus—to participate in the play of differing measures, where meaning emerges from a deference to difference rather than a resolution of difference.

The Blue Note: Errant Polyphonics, Off-the-Mark and Beside-the-Point

The blue note, with its expressive wavering and refusal of tonal accuracy and precision, challenges symphonic consonance by embodying spectral drift—polyphonic dissonances that begin elsewhere, bending towards and wavering around the note but refusing fixed resolution. It verges on the "off-key" while gesturing toward the "on-key," defying the colonial musical ideal of perfect pitch.

Colonial science mirrors this obsession with accuracy and precision, dividing error into random error (noise) and systematic error (bias). Random error is seen as accidental deviation; systematic error, as a bias to be judged desirable or undesirable. Both assume that error must be corrected in the pursuit of truth.

The blue note unsettles this logic. It blurs the line between random and systematic, between accident and design. It does not assume there to be a target missed due to error but, rather, finds expressive tension in the manner of missing and drifting away from and around a target—opening new possibilities rather than closing them.

This is the errantry Glissant describes: not a failure to make one's point but an affirmation of the significance of what is beside the point to the significance of the point itself. Where colonial science polices deviation, decolonial science embraces errantry as a condition of being in relation. To drift, to waver, to resist hitting the mark and sticking to the point is not a methodological failure but a way of being-in-the-world more ethically and more aesthetically.

The Ring Shout: Improvisation and the Observer Becoming the Observed

The ring shout challenges the authority of the composer and conductor by way of a participatory structure where knowledge emerges relationally. In this Afro-diasporic practice, dancers, singers, and players move collectively in a circular formation. Call-and-response blurs the line between performer and audience. Knowledge arises not from fixed roles but through confluent exchanges of responsibility, losing one role and finding the other, again and again, time after time.

This challenges the colonial scientific paradigm of detached observation. The colonial observer stands apart as composer and conductor of experiments, rendering the world passive for analysis, while the ring shout collapses this distance. The observer/listener becomes the observed/player as participation deepens—drawn into the rhythm, responding to the call, becoming part of the music's unfolding.

We have already noted how African music depends on the tension of losing and finding the beat and the note. In the ring shout, the observer/listener "completes" the music by becoming an observed/player, clapping, singing, and moving "on-key" and "on-beat" in response to leading calls from those already cast as observed/players who are "off-key" and "off-beat." Sense-making is distributed, emergent, and shared.

The deeper one participates, however, the more errant one becomes, as one is tasked with playing "off-key" and "off-beat" in order to invite anyone who finds themselves in the role of observer/listener to make the transition into observed/player, clapping, singing, and moving "on-key" and "on-beat." The fixed roles dissolve as each participant contributes polymetric and polyphonic variations, destabilizing the authority of a single voice. Mastery dissolves into confluence. Knowledge arises not from control but from the pulse of collective, unfolding relations

Decolonial science mirrors this structure. It refuses the colonial fixation on mastering the object of knowledge. Instead, it recognizes that to know is to be in relation, where observer and observed blur into a shared pulse, pitch, and timbre of participation. Knowledge, like the rhythms of the ring shout, emerges from the confluence of relations—not imposed from above but co-created through call and response.

Decolonial Science: the Improvisation of Errant Relations

The break beat, the blue note, and the ring shout offer sonic paradigms for rethinking knowledge production beyond colonial control. The polymetric break beat resists the monometric, affirming the generativity of dissensus. The polyphonic blue note bends the boundaries of correctness, challenging the symphonic demand for harmonic unity. The improvised participatory antiphonies of the ring shout dissolve the authority of the composer and conductor, transforming knowledge into a participatory, call-and-response practice.

While colonial science seeks consensus, resolution, and mastery, decolonial science pulses with errantry— multiple measures in tension, voices in polyphonic dissonance, roles shifting in improvisatory confluences. This is not a rejection of structure but a refusal of epistemic enclosure—an affirmation that knowledge is relational, participatory, and always incomplete.

To practice decolonial science, then, is not merely to critique colonial paradigms but to engage differently with the rhythms of the world. It is to be part of the break, the drift, the call-and-response—to participate in the errant unfolding of knowledge as a living, breathing confluence of relations.

FUGITIVE EROTICS

INTRODUCTION
Desire at the Crossroads

The erotic is a measure between the beginnings of our sense of self and the chaos of our strongest feelings. It is an internal sense of satisfaction to which, once we have experienced it, we know we can aspire. For having experienced the fullness of this depth of feeling and recognizing its power, in honor and self-respect we can require no less of ourselves.

It is never easy to demand the most from ourselves, from our lives, from our work. To encourage excellence is to go beyond the encouraged mediocrity of our society. But giving in to the fear of feeling and working to capacity is a luxury only the unintentional can afford, and the unintentional are those who do not wish to guide their own destinies.

This internal requirement toward excellence which we learn from the erotic must not be misconstrued as demanding the impossible from ourselves nor from others. Such a demand incapacitates everyone in the process. For the erotic is not a question only of what we do; it is a question of how acutely and fully we can feel in the doing. Once we know the extent to which we are capable of feeling that sense of satisfaction and completion, we can then observe which of our various life endeavors brings us closest to that fullness.

—Audre Lorde, from "The Uses of the Erotic" (1978)

Imagine yourself imprisoned. In the shadow of confinement, your mind reaches for freedom. You picture the beach: the warmth of sand yielding to your feet, the briny aroma of the sea carried by the wind, the tide lapping gently at your ankles. In this dreamscape, your lover stands beside you, their smile as endless as the horizon. For a fleeting moment, the world feels whole.

This vision does not linger as a fantasy; it sparks a defiant insistence that you will escape. You and your fellow prisoners conspire in low whispers, but when the digging begins, so too does the sound. Voices steadily rise, no longer so careful—work songs echo in the clandestine tunnels, each strike of the earth carrying the promise of flight. The sound is not merely accompaniment but refusal in its own right, reverberating through the passages in waves of shared resolve. Improvisation takes hold: a shout, a curse, a laugh, a stomp, weaving together into a din that seems capable of undoing the world around you.

At last, the riot erupts. Bodies surge and collide, voices reaching a fever pitch as if calling to spirits from beyond. Amid the commotion, you seize your chance, breaking into the night. You and your comrades become a single, pulsing formation—an ensemble of treason and tumult, bent on calling the reality of the prison's walls into question. You run as if the rhythm itself, like an animal spirit, has seized your limbs.

But the world outside mocks your dream. You are pursued relentlessly. The lover whose smile once sustained your hope has moved on, their warmth now a warning as they threaten to turn you in. When you finally reach the beach that lived in your dreams, it is unrecognizable. Fenced off and patrolled by armed guards, the sand is claimed by a private equity firm breaking ground for a luxury hotel. The tide is no longer yours to touch.

Was it all for naught? The planning, the discipline, the rebellion—was it wasted? Did your efforts crumble under the weight of this betrayal? That depends. Did the discipline hone your strength, sharpening your resolve, or did it punish your body and drain your spirit? Did the planning and the riot forge an ensemble, binding you to your fellow prisoners in shared defiance, or did it alienate you, leaving resentment in your wake? Were the songs, the shouts, and the dance of your escape mere gestures, or did they inspire you to a new way of being?

If the noise of rebellion held no joy, no beauty, no strengthening, no communion, then it was for nothing. The dream failed, and the end betrayed you. But if the music thrummed with life—if the breaking forged bonds stronger than fear—then it was everything. The break itself was the realization, the transformation. Desire was never on the distant horizon but in the shout that refused to be silenced, in the footsteps pounding through the night, life-sustaining like a heartbeat. In that case, your desires were realized in the means, not the end.

Fugitive Erotics is the practice of finding pleasure, strength, and connection in the act of breaking, of escaping—not to a destination but in the rhythm of the movement. It reclaims liberation as an ongoing practice, not a fixed horizon.

This essay explores erotic desire as a dynamic, world-making force that defies containment and (re-)creates sensuality and intimacy in the break. Rejecting the notion of desire as mere individual longing, it reframes desire as—a force that makes things happen—emerging at the crossroads of systemic violence, relational entanglement, and the in-/re-surgencies of the flesh. By tracing desire across three interconnected scales—the sub-molecular, molecular, and molar—this work reveals how domination dismembers bodies and relations while also illuminating practices that transform these fractures into sites of repair and liberation.

At the sub-molecular scale, desire resides in the visceral, the immediate, and the partial. Drawing on Hortense Spillers' conception of "flesh" as a site for rites of breakage and repair, this scale exposes the ways colonial violence dismembers the body, yet also reveals the flesh's refusal to be fully disciplined. The rhythmic hunger of the mouth, the pulse of the anus, the searching gaze of the eyes—all defy coherence, reclaiming sensation as a site of in-/re-surgency. Afro-diasporic rites involving drumming, chanting, and spirit possession transform the profaned flesh into a sacred vessel, where invisibility becomes a force and immediacy becomes resistance.

The molecular scale examines desire as relational, operating within the bonds between co-constituted bodies. Here, domination is exposed as a force that seeks to sever and exploit, while Afro-diasporic rites demonstrate the radical creativity of re-bonding. The ring-shout, for example, choreographs dismembered bodies into rhythmic, communal resistance. In these spaces, brokenness is not a deficit but a generative force, where relationships are remade and solidarity thrives amidst structural violences.

At the molar scale, desire confronts the abstractions of systemic power—colonial hierarchies, administrative regimes, and racial taxonomies—that seek to reduce bodies to bits of data and codify identities for extraction and control. Yet Afro-diasporic practices disrupt these mechanisms, composing fugitive spaces of intimacy, opacity, and collectivity. The sonic ecologies of Black electronic dance musics—their bass materialisms (Steve Goodman) and maroon choreographies (fahima ife)—hack molar architectures to produce resonant fields of subversion. Through rhythm and relationality, these practices generate portals of refusal and refuge, where life escapes capture and reassembles itself otherwise.

Across these scales, Fugitive Erotics illuminates how Afro-diasporic rites transform breakdowns into breakthroughs. Under the weight of colonial violence, the dismemberment of the Black body gave rise to practices that transformed brokeness into relational creativity. Vodou, Candomblé, Hoodoo, and their kin—including the embodied ecstasies of Black electronic dance musics—offer models of fugitivity where rhythm, intimacy, and movement become acts of remembrance and defiance.

By inhabiting the breaks—those sites where power falters and life can be reconfigured—through ritual, rhythm, and refusal, Fugitive Erotics calls us to reclaim desire as a force of in-/re-surgent creativity. Liberation is not a destination; it is an active, tidalectic rhythm—the ebbing and flowing—of life in the process of breaking free.

THE SUB_MOLECULAR
THE SENSUAL

The sub-molecular scale is a realm that precedes, exceeds, and succeeds the existence of the integrated individual or unified body. Indeed, at this level, there is no cohesive entity that can be termed a body. Instead, there is a constellation of broke down parts—organs and drives—acting autonomously or in fleeting coordination. This is the domain of flesh, as conceptualized by Hortense Spillers in "Mama's Baby, Papa's Maybe: An American Grammar Book" (1987). Flesh operates as a dynamic field of potential, resisting efforts to impose coherence or integration. It is raw, impulsive, and driven toward satisfaction.

At this scale, each organ functions as a partial subject, animated by its own specific drives and seeking satisfaction through confluences with the external world. The flesh is never static; it is perpetually in motion—sensing, responding, consuming, and releasing. Desire at the sub-molecular scale is visceral and immediate, unfolding in the momentary coupling of organs with the objects that satisfy their drives.

The Drives and Their Sensations
An Incomplete Catalogue

The Mouth and Throat

The mouth is drawn toward what can be sucked, swallowed, and savored. The warmth of milk, the texture of skin, the rhythmic flow of fluids—all these satisfy the mouth's primal hunger. The sensation of a nipple or the resistance encountered by a bite connects the mouth to its object, creating a fleeting moment of satisfaction.

The Anus

The anus exists in a perpetual tension between clenching and release. It is drawn toward objects that offer resistance—something to hold in—or surrender, as in the release of waste. The drive of the anus is tactile and rhythmic, finding satisfaction in the controlled play of tightening and loosening.

The Eyes

Always seeking, the eyes are insatiable in their desire to consume the visual world. Light, color, motion, and contrast captivate them, drawing their focus in endless shifts. The satisfaction of the scopic drive is fleeting, tied to the discovery of something new or the lingering allure of a particularly striking sight.

The Ears

The ears attune themselves to the vibrations of sound, drawn to whispers, melodies, and cacophonies alike. Whether soothed by a lullaby or startled by a sudden noise, the ears are compelled by the rhythm and resonance of their surrounds.

The Nose

The nose, ever curious, plunges into the world of scents. It seeks the earthy, the floral, the pungent, the faint trace of a familiar smell. Scents provoke memory and desire, drawing the nose toward the lingering, elusive satisfaction of something just out of reach.

The Tongue

The tongue craves the interplay of taste and texture, delighting in the salty, the sweet, the bitter, the savory, and the sour. It revels in the tactile pleasure of food as much as its flavor, exploring every surface it encounters.

The Hands

The hands, restless and tactile, are driven to touch, hold, and manipulate. They crave the solidity of objects, the pliability of skin, the sensation of pressing and shaping. The hands find satisfaction in action, in the feel of material resistance or compliance.

The Sex

Charged with a yearning for orgasm, the sex organs are driven by the interplay of stimulation and release. Their satisfaction is rhythmic, a crescendo of tension that seeks fulfillment in moments of release.

The Nerves

The nervous system, though overarching, remains fragmented in its attempts to coordinate these drives. It seeks to satisfy them either simultaneously or sequentially, striving for rhythmic alignment. Its efforts create connections—linking the mouth to a nipple, the eyes to its sight, and the hands to its touch. However, this coordination is always incomplete; it assembles organs into partial, patchy arrangements rather than forming a whole, unified body. The result is a fleeting choreography of sensations and responses, never achieving full integration.

Dynamics of Desire at the Sub-Molecular Scale

Desire at the sub-molecular scale is immediate and sensual, unfolding in moments of coupling between partial subjects (organs) and partial objects (the things that satisfy their drives). The process is ephemeral—each coupling provides only temporary satisfaction, leaving the organ ready to seek again.

Consider the mouth meeting the nipple: the warmth and texture create a momentary sense of completion, but the drive reasserts itself as soon as the flow of milk ceases. The eyes fixate on a flash of light, captivated, only to shift their focus to the next compelling sight. The hands grip an object, feel its resistance, and move on to explore another.

This tidalectics of seeking, finding, and seeking again defines desire at this scale. It is an unending dance of sensation and response, where satisfaction is always partial and fleeting. The sub-molecular scale resists permanence; it is a realm of immediacy, where drives act independently, sometimes in consensus, often in dissensus.

The Sensuality of Dismemberment

The sub-molecular scale invites us to imagine flesh not as a coherent, unified body but as an incoherent assemblage of erogenous zones seeking sensation. Each organ engages with the world in its own way, creating a field of sensual experience that is rich, chaotic, and deeply embodied. This dismemberment is not a deficiency but a form of abundance—an openness to the world that allows for endless possibilities of confluence and desire.

At this level, flesh becomes a site of pure potential, where the drives of the mouth, hands, eyes, and sex organs converge and diverge unpredictably. The satisfaction of one drive may amplify the yearning of another, creating a dynamic interplay of sensations that resists resolution. Flesh, as Spillers describes it, is not a static substrate but a living, responsive field—a realm where desire is continually reborn through the interplay of organs and objects.

This chaotic sensuality forms the foundation for more complex scales of desire. Yet it also stands alone as a domain that shapes the most intimate and immediate aspects of how we experience the world.

THE MOLECULAR
THE RELATIONAL

At the sub-molecular scale, partial drives and organs function independently, resisting coherence or integration. By contrast, the molecular scale centers relationality. Here, the scattered assemblages of flesh and drives begin to align, the coordination of organs and responses form organized bodies and bonds among them. Desire, no longer confined to the visceral interactions of partial subjects and objects, emerges as inherently relational—shaped by mutual engagement and, importantly, by systems of power and domination.

Unlike the sub-molecular scale, which resists cohesion, the molecular scale introduces a provisional form of coherence—not as the unity of an individual body, but as an interplay between multiple bodies, each composed of multiple organs and each contributing to the creation and maintenance of relationships. These bonds do not eliminate sub-molecular fragmentation; rather, they channel it into rhythmic confluences influenced by cultural, systemic, and environmental forces. Molecular relationality necessitates at least two bodies, each composed of interconnected organs. A solitary body, deprived of connection, gradually reverts to its dismembered state, slipping back into the sub-molecular realm of disarticulated flesh.

Critically, these relational bodies need not be of the same species—or even living. Molecular bonds exceed anthropocentric frameworks, extending to the elemental, vegetal, animal, and ecological others that shape and sustain life. The winds, rains, seas, soils, clouds, sun, and moon resonate with elemental rhythms; trees, shrubs, herbs, grasses, mosses, lichens, and fungi pulse with vegetal rhythms; birds, insects, fish, reptiles, amphibians, and mammals embody animal rhythms. Beyond this, forests, woodlands, and watersheds—ecological assemblages composed of elemental, vegetal, and animal components—move with intricate, co-constituted rhythms of their own.

These rhythms are not static but dynamic, requiring continuous negotiation and response. Human bodies, embedded within these larger ecologies, form bonds with the non-human others through which life unfolds. A body drinks from and bathes in a river, breathes in and dances with the wind, climbs and sways to the rhythms of trees, and follows the lunar tides. These interactions reveal that molecular relationality is not confined to human sociality but emerges as a process of becoming-with—the co-creation of life through the intricate choreography of beings and forces.

FORMS OF MOLECULAR BONDS

Molecular bonds are far from neutral; they reflect underlying dynamics of power, agency, and reciprocity—or their violent absence. Within systems of domination, such as colonial or enslaving contexts, these bonds are fundamentally shaped by relations of exploitation and coercion, dismembering some individuals to serve as tools that satisfy the desires and purposes of others.

POLARIZING BONDS

Polarizing bonds occur when one individual is compelled to objectify themselves—or is forcibly objectified—for the sensory engagement of another. In such relations, one person becomes the object—a sight to behold, a sound to hear, a touch to feel—while the other assumes the role of active subject, the one who senses and consumes. These bonds are not neutral but reproduce hierarchies of power, as seen in colonial systems where domination and exploitation dictated relational dynamics.

For enslaved people, these polarizing bonds were not merely imposed but violently reinforced to strip them of bodily autonomy and personhood. The enslaved were reduced to flesh—a collection of organs belonging to others, with no cohesive body of their own. They existed as broken down parts—tools to labor, reproduce, or satisfy the desires of the enslaver. Their hands, genitals, wombs, and other bodily parts became appendages of the enslaver's body, severed from their original agency and subordinated to the machinery of colonial exploitation.

White colonial masculinity engages in polarizing bonds by appropriating the organs of the enslaved as extensions of itself, enabling it to sense and control others in the world. This masculinity is defined by an active, consuming subjectivity that transforms the enslaved into tools of perception and mastery. For instance, the muscles, hands, and genitals of the enslaved are appropriated to work, touch, or (re-)produce on behalf of the colonizer. In this configuration, the enslaved are broken down into instruments that amplify the colonial masculine's capacity to act and perceive, reinforcing its dominant subject position.

White colonial femininity, by contrast, appropriates the bodies of the enslaved to position itself as the focal point of sensory engagement—to be seen, admired, and affirmed by others. The enslaved body, irrespective of gender, becomes an accessory that enhances the colonial feminine's visibility, desirability, and perceived refinement. The labor of enslaved individuals, both men and women, was essential to constructing beauty, comfort, and domestic order, elevating colonial femininity into a spectacle of grace and civility. This dynamic frames the flesh taken from enslaved men and women alike as extensions of the colonial feminine form, subordinated to amplify its allure and significance, while simultaneously concealing the violence intrinsic to this relationship.

These distinctions reveal a relational polarity that underpinned colonial systems of oppression: white colonial masculinity as the subject who senses and acts, and white colonial femininity as the object sensed and idealized. Both, however, relied on the violent appropriation of the enslaved body, breaking it down into tools that supported the machinery of colonial domination and erasure. This system not only defined the roles of enslaver and enslaved but also constructed gendered hierarchies that remain deeply entrenched in social and cultural relations today.

Colonial relations with non-human others mirrored the dynamics of polarizing bonds between colonizers and the enslaved. Land, animals, and ecosystems were subjected to the same processes of dismemberment and appropriation, treated as commodities to be consumed, controlled, and exploited. Just as the enslaved were reduced to flesh, stripped of agency, and broken down into tools of labor and reproduction, non-human entities were reduced to "natural resources"—their rhythms, capacities, and relational networks severed to serve colonial extraction and domination. Indeed, the flesh of the enslaved was, in fact, just one such "natural resource" amongst others.

Colonial masculinity imposed mastery over non-human others, transforming rivers into conduits for trade, forests into commodities for logging, and animals into machines for labor or trophies for display. This dynamic reinforced the colonizer's subjectivity as one who acts, consumes, and dominates, mirroring the reduction of enslaved people to tools that extended the colonizer's sensory and productive reach.

Colonial femininity, similarly, appropriated non-human others to enhance its visibility and desirability. Gardens, exotic plants, and domesticated animals were curated to perform an aesthetic of refinement and civility. The labor required to maintain these displays, often performed by enslaved individuals, was erased, just as the ecological costs of extraction were hidden beneath the veneer of colonial progress and beauty. Non-human others, like the enslaved, were instrumentalized to uphold the spectacle of white colonial femininity.

COMMUNIZING BONDS

In contrast to polarizing bonds, communizing bonds are characterized by mutuality and reciprocity. These bonds generate possibilities for connection that elude domination, enabling individuals to share and co-constitute relational dynamics. Communizing bonds function in two primary ways: by allowing bodies to alternate in rhythm between the roles of subject and object, or by creating conditions where individuals inhabit both roles simultaneously and in sync. In the latter case, one person senses while also being sensed, seeing while being seen, or touching while being touched, producing a shared and overlapping relational field that resists the asymmetries of polarizing dynamics.

In communizing bonds, the dismemberment of the sub-molecular scale is not erased but embraced as part of a dynamic interplay. This interplay honors the autonomy and rhythms of each constituent part, weaving them into a cohesive, co-constituted relationship. These bonds foster the sharing of agency, wherein bodies both give and receive, sense and are sensed, opening pathways for confluent engagements that challenge the fixed hierarchies imposed by polarizing systems.

However, colonial systems worked systematically to suppress and replace communizing bonds with polarizing dynamics. The enslavement and commodification of African peoples sought to obliterate reciprocal relationality, ensuring that enslaved individuals primarily existed as objects of extraction, stripped of autonomy and relational complexity. Communizing bonds, which might have allowed for mutual care and shared agency, were deliberately undermined. The enslaved were prohibited from forming robust relational fabrics that could sustain resistance, resilience, or entanglement. Instead, their relational capacities were reoriented toward exploitation, becoming tools of domination rather than connection.

This suppression of communizing bonds was not incidental but central to the colonial project. Relationality itself became a site of control, as systems of racial capitalism restructured the social fabric to prioritize extraction over intimacy, dismemberment over relation. The colonizer's success relied on isolating bodies—human and non-human alike—disrupting their ability to form dynamic, reciprocal networks that could challenge the machinery of domination.

BODY-SNATCHING AND ORGAN-HARVESTING

Colonial and enslaving systems did not merely exploit enslaved individuals for labor or reproduction; they appropriated their very bodies, transforming them into tools for the colonial apparatus. Enslaved people were reduced to flesh—a collection of organs harvested and reassembled to serve the desires of others. This process, aptly described as body-snatching and organ-harvesting, denied the enslaved any claim to their own bodies.

THE ENSLAVED AS HANDS

Enslaved men and women were reduced to hands, alienated from their agency and transformed into instruments of labor. These hands no longer served the desires of the enslaved but became extensions of the plow, the hoe, or the loom, severed and subordinated to the rhythms of colonial production.

THE ENSLAVED MAN AS COCK

Enslaved men were reduced to cocks, their sexuality commodified and weaponized. Their reproductive capacities were appropriated to produce future generations of enslaved laborers. At the same time, enslaved men were hypersexualized, their sexuality portrayed as dangerous and subject to strict control.

Thus, the cock became both a tool of reproduction and an object of fear, its purpose defined by the needs of the colonizer.

The Enslaved Woman as Womb and Cunt

Enslaved women were reduced to wombs and cunts, their reproductive and sexual agency stripped away entirely. As wombs, they were forced to bear children who were treated as commodities, severing any bond of personhood or lineage. Their wombs became resources for the enslaving system, manufactories for new fleshy parts to perpetuate the cycle of exploitation. As cunts, they were subjected to sexual violence that served the dual purpose of asserting control and satisfying the colonizer's desires. Their bodies were claimed as sites of both reproductive labor and sexual consumption, rendering their most intimate capacities alienable and exploitable. The enslaved woman, reduced to these organs, existed only as a vessel for the colonizer's needs.

The Enslaver as Body-Snatcher

The enslaver effectively became a body-snatcher, appropriating the organs of the enslaved and integrating them into their own systems of labor, reproduction, and consumption. The hands of the enslaved worked the fields, the wombs produced offspring for the system, and the cunts and cocks were exploited for sexual gratification and control. The enslaved were denied autonomy over their organs, which were no longer theirs but redefined as tools belonging to the colonizer's body.

Organ-Harvesting as Dismemberment

The process of organ-harvesting fractured the enslaved body, severing hands, wombs, cunts, and cocks from the individuals they once belonged to—individuals bound in reciprocal relation—and repurposing them as discrete functions within the colonial libidinal economy. This dismemberment deepened the dehumanization of the enslaved, rendering them not as whole persons capable of relation, but as a scattered assemblage of parts, stripped of autonomy and connection.

The enslaver's focus on specific organs—hands for labor, wombs for reproduction, cunts for sexual consumption, and stud cocks for controlled breeding—illustrates the instrumental logic of the system. The enslaved body was treated not as a person but as a resource, its parts harvested, commodified, and reassembled to sustain the colonial apparatus.

BETRAYED BY THE FLESH

Enslaved men and women experienced a profound sense of betrayal by their own organs, which acted in defiance of their autonomy under the pressures of domination. Their hands grasped tools and labored to sustain systems that denied their personhood and humanity. Their cocks and cunts, commodified and weaponized, participated in acts of sexual coupling and reproduction that perpetuated cycles of enslavement, often without consent or agency. Their wombs bore children who were claimed by the enslaving system, severing the possibility of kinship on their own terms. In these moments, the drives of their organs became tools for perpetuating their oppression, rendering them estranged from their own flesh.

This betrayal originated in the sub-molecular drives of the flesh, where dismembered organs acted with a will of their own, fulfilling functions disconnected from the desires or intentions of the individual. The organs, reduced to fungible utilities, satisfied drives and performed functions, but in ways that deepened their alienation. In this dismemberment, enslaved individuals endured a bodily disintegration that reflected and reinforced the larger systems of exploitation and control they were forced to navigate.

The Molecular Scale as a Site of Domination

At the molecular scale, relations between individuals were fundamentally shaped by the dynamics of domination. The bonds forged by enslaved individuals were violently reoriented and torn asunder to serve the desires of the colonizer, systematically extinguishing any possibility of mutuality or reciprocity. The processes of body-snatching and organ-harvesting ensured that the enslaved existed not as autonomous beings but as replaceable parts of the colonial machine.

Where communizing bonds survived or emerged, they enacted moments of resistance and relational integrity. Such bonds enabled enslaved individuals to commune with one another—and, at times, even with their enslavers—as both subject and object, or to simultaneously inhabit both roles, generating fugitive spaces of mutuality that unsettled the totalizing logic of colonial domination. Yet these openings were always under siege, as the colonial apparatus labored to extinguish reciprocity and replace it with rigid, polarizing hierarchies.

By examining the molecular scale, we uncover how desire, labor, and relationality were reconstructed to sustain systems of control. The enslaved, reduced to organs without bodies, became sites of profound dismemberment and disintegration. Their relations were distorted, their body parts appropriated, and their capacity for autonomy and reciprocity diminished, revealing the profound violence embedded in these systems of exploitation. Yet, within this dismemberment, the potential for communizing bonds persisted, offering glimpses of relational resistance against the totalizing forces of domination.

Resistance on the Molecular Scale

Resistance on the molecular scale emerged through the coordination of organs to form communizing bonds amongst fugitive bodies that countered the polarizing dynamics of colonial systems. In conditions of enslavement and systemic oppression, Black people developed ways to transform their broken down flesh into sites of agency. These efforts created communizing bonds that embraced mutuality and reciprocity, subverting the logic of domination that sought to reduce their bodies to tools of labor or objects of exploitation.

Practices like Capoeira in Brazil exemplify this resistance. Concealed as dance that might amuse the master but rooted in martial discipline, Capoeira enabled enslaved individuals to train for defense while cultivating communizing bonds through rhythm and shared movement. Within its fluid choreography, participants alternated and combined the roles of subject and object, shifting confluently between displaying and sensing—generating fugitive spaces of mutuality that resisted the polarizing dynamics of domination.

Black dance, music, and call-and-response vernaculars more broadly fostered relational spaces outside the logic of domination. Underground forms of expression reclaimed severed body parts into communizing acts of joy, remembrance, and (re-)creative repair. Movement and rhythm reoriented polarizing bonds enforced by colonial systems, enabling individuals to form dynamic, co-constituted relations. Whether alternating or simultaneously embodying roles of sensing and being sensed, participants created a shared presence that subverted the isolating and objectifying forces of domination.

THE MOLAR
THE SYSTEMIC

At the molar scale, desire and relationality are shaped by systems of administration designed to govern populations as aggregates. Borrowing from chemistry, the term "molar" reflects processes of averaging and standardization applied to large masses—methods that reduce individual variations into manageable statistical identities. Just as molar mass in chemistry averages variations among molecules, molar administration treats individuals as "more or less identical," abstracting them into classifications, roles, and functions within collective frameworks. These systems do not merely describe—they actively produce the standardizations they claim to observe, enforcing conformity to institutional norms and goals.

ABSTRACTION IN MOLAR ADMINISTRATION

Molar administration operates through two dominant forms of abstraction: visual and symbolic. Visual abstraction maps populations onto observable grids of control, while symbolic abstraction, largely through language, assigns fixed identities and functions. These abstractions not only simplify complexity but actively shape and regulate individual and collective behaviors, often privileging certain senses and modes of relation over others.

Going further, by prioritizing written language over oral language and, in turn, prioritizing typographic writing over calligraphic writing, molar systems combine visual and symbolic abstraction into a singular apparatus of control. Typographic writing fixes meaning and identity into static forms and, as a visual medium, it privileges sight over other sensory modes of engagement. The oral, with its reliance on sound, resonance, and rhythm, and the calligraphic, with its emotive and choreographed gesturality, offer more dynamic and relational modes of communication that resist the rigidity of typographic abstraction. Molar systems frequently subordinate oral and calligraphic traditions, reducing them to secondary or illegitimate forms of knowledge in favor of the typographic written word, which aligns more seamlessly with administrative needs.

Visual Abstraction: The Dominance of the Eye
At the molar scale, vision asserts dominance as the primary sense, shaping both sub-molecular drives and molecular bonds that structure human relations.

Vision's capacity to operate at a distance enables the mapping of individuals within spaces of control, much like points on a Cartesian grid. This visual logic transforms bodies into objects of observation and administration, reducing them to locations, displacements, and functions. The black mirrors of social media and electronic surveillance epitomize this dominance, amplifying the role of the eye in rendering individuals hyper-visible for categorization, consumption, and regulation. Profiles, metrics, and data points become modern equivalents of bodies dissected and abstracted by the gaze.

This dominance of the eye today has historical precedents in anthropometrics and race science, which elevated vision as the authoritative sense for classifying and controlling bodies. These colonial pseudo-sciences relied on the visual measurement and comparison of human features, turning bodies into objects of scrutiny and taxonomy. The eye, as the arbiter of truth, reduced individuals to physical attributes presumed to be representative of deeper truths about identity, behavior, and value. This framework of visual dominance not only racialized bodies but also established the foundations for contemporary surveillance and social media, where the gaze fragments individuals into data points and consumable imagery.

Visual primacy reorients relational dynamics, privileging the detached, distanced operations of sight over the intimate, multi-sensory engagements of touch, smell, and sound. Vision's detachment enables the abstraction of human interactions, subordinating the sensory interplay that fosters erotic proximity, depth, and connection. In social media, this manifests as the demand for individuals to curate themselves into stereotyped visual content for validation and recognition. In surveillance, the gaze renders bodies as targets of scrutiny and control. Both systems extend the logic of visual dominance, eroding embodied and multi-sensory ways of relating.

Molecular bonds, which might otherwise form through intimate, multi-sensory interactions, are increasingly mediated and distorted by the relentless demands of visibility. The eye's dominance, rooted in the pseudo-scientific practices of anthropometrics and race science, underpins these systems. Social media and surveillance exploit this legacy, dismembering human relations into visual performances and trackable bits, reinforcing hierarchies of power while diminishing the potential for unmediated, fully embodied connections.

SYMBOLIC ABSTRACTION: FIXING IDENTITIES

Complementing visual abstraction, symbolic abstraction operates through language to assign generalized identities to individuals and populations. Denotative language forms the backbone of molar administration, filtering the confluences of lived experience and channeling them into categories like race, gender, and class. These abstractions function like algebraic equations in a geometric framework, defining relations between fixed points and reducing individuals to functions.

Typographic writing, as a tool of symbolic abstraction, intensifies the influence of visual logic by fixing identity into static, repeatable forms. This rigidity contrasts with the oral, which is ephemeral, contextually resonant, and reliant on tone and mutual engagement, and with the calligraphic, which is inherently embodied and burdened by the singular, gestural traces of its creation. Typographic abstraction erases this embodied dynamism, reducing identities to fixed representations. Racialized categories, for example, reduce Blackness to predefined, stereotyped functions—labor, hypersexuality, or criminality. These symbolic abstractions do not merely reflect social realities; they actively construct and enforce them, embedding hierarchies of power and domination within systems of representation.

In concert with visual abstraction, typographic abstraction imposes a static framework that aligns individuals with the functional demands of administrative power, suppressing relational forms of life that resist codification. By privileging sight and rigid symbolic systems, molar administration consolidates its authority through reduction—compressing the living, shifting complexities of human experience into legible categories designed for surveillance, extraction, and control. The plantation ledgers that once quantified the value of enslaved labor have not vanished; they have mutated into today's data-driven apparatuses—tracking incarceration, reproducing racial typologies, and embedding structural inequalities into healthcare systems, employment metrics, educational access, and the algorithms that dictate visibility, validation, and disposability across digital platforms.

The Limits of Molar Administration

Even as molar systems exert immense power, they cannot fully contain the complexities of life that persist and resist at the molecular and sub-molecular scales. The bonds of flesh and intimacy exceed the constraints imposed by abstraction, exposing the inherent limits of visual and symbolic control.

Take, for example, "the Talk" Black parents give their children about systemic racism. While shaped by the brutal realities of anti-Black violence—measured and perpetuated by molar systems—this exchange defies abstraction. Rooted in shared feeling and communal resilience, it fosters a molecular intimacy that molar systems cannot capture or contain. These bonds, forged in the crucible of oppression, offer an entanglement that eludes the mechanisms of control.

Even in the harshest conditions, enslaved individuals resisted the polarizing dynamics of molar systems through collective practices that reasserted relationality and agency. The Afro-diasporic ring shout, for instance, became a radical form of worship and resistance. Rooted in African spiritual traditions, this communal, circular movement synchronized clapping, stomping, and singing into a collective force. The ring shout's improvisational nature rejected the rigidity of molar abstraction, privileging proximity, sound, and embodied interaction. This practice re-centered the flesh as a site of defiance, reclaiming agency through shared presence and rhythm.

Communal practices like the ring shout disrupted the isolating dominance of visual and symbolic abstraction, privileging connection over commodification. These spaces of molecular resistance re-forged broke down relations, nurturing living, resilient bonds that challenged the erasure imposed by molar systems. By elluding the frameworks of abstraction, these practices illuminated the systemic failures of molar systems to dominate the fullness of human complexity.

Toward a Critical Understanding of the Molar

To challenge the dominance of molar systems, we must expose the interplay of visual and symbolic abstraction that underpins them. This requires reclaiming the sensory and relational dimensions they seek to pervert to colonial ends and fostering spaces where life can resist the logic of administration.

Resistance lies not only in rejecting molar abstractions but in reimagining relationality itself. This means valuing the oral alongside the written, the tactile alongside the visual, and the dynamic alongside the fixed. By cultivating spaces that prioritize connection as (re-)creative repair, we can subvert the mechanisms of control that seek to disintegrate and standardize human experience.

The work of fugitive erotics is to inhabit the breaks in molar systems, to nurture relationality in spaces they cannot fully capture. It is to reclaim invisibility and ineffability, reconfiguring them into living, in-/re-surgent forms that refuse to be reduced, measured, or controlled. Through these acts of reclamation, life asserts its vitality against the totalizing forces of the molar, making space for new possibilities of connection and liberation.

THE COLONIAL ORDER OF SEXUALITY
Libidinal Economy Across Scales

To recapitulate and integrate the insights developed thus far, we now turn to the colonial order of sexuality—a system of dominance that dismembers bodies, distorts relations, and codifies hierarchies to sustain its rule. Within this regime, white men are positioned as sovereign gazers and possessors; white women as idealized objects of purity and value; colonized men as hypersexual threats and laboring instruments; and colonized women as paradoxically disposable yet indispensable—reduced to reproductive and sexual functions. Through appropriation, polarization, and abstraction, this order manipulates intimacy across all three scales—sub-molecular, molecular, and molar—embedding its logics of control into flesh, relation, and systemic structure. Even acts that appear subversive, such as interracial or same-sex relations, often reproduce these underlying logics, revealing the persistent adaptability and resilience of the colonial framework.

SUB-MOLECULAR SCALE: DISMEMBERMENT AND SENSORY APPROPRIATION

At the sub-molecular scale, the colonial order targets the most intimate, visceral aspects of desire, breaking down bodies into organs and drives that are appropriated and redefined to uphold systems of power. Desire is stripped of its coherence, with sensory pleasures redirected into tools for domination and dispossession.

WHITE MEN

The gaze of white men dominates the sub-molecular scale, functioning as the primary organ of appropriation. Through their eyes, colonized bodies are dismembered into consumable parts—erogenous zones, laboring hands, or reproductive capacities—stripped of autonomy and reassembled within the colonial libidinal economy. This visual dominance asserts white masculinity as the active subject, consuming and controlling the bodies of others. Moreover, the white man appropriates the gazes of others—white women, colonized men, and colonized women—transforming their eyes into extensions of his own body, tools for panoptic surveillance and pornoscopic voyeurism. The eyes of white women, colonized men, and colonized women are co-opted to see the world, and themselves, through the white man's perspective, betraying their autonomy as they replicate his vision and uphold his dominance.

WHITE WOMEN

White women's bodies are subjected to the dismembering gaze as well, but they are re-assembled and re-positioned as objects of value and purity within the colonial order. Their breasts, butts, thighs, and lips are fetishized as symbols of desirability, rendered hyper-visible within a framework that preserves their status as possessions of white men. This dismemberment underscores their objectification while ensuring their alignment with patriarchal and racial hierarchies.

COLONIZED MEN

Colonized men are reduced to symbols of impotence and emasculation or hypersexuality and dangerous potency, their bodies commodified as trivialized or spectacularized phallic objects. The colonial gaze appropriates their genitals as emblems of threat or fetish, perpetuating narratives of deviance and subjugation.

Colonized Women

Colonized women are paradoxically rendered disposable yet indispensable within the sub-molecular scale. Their bodies are reduced to cunts and wombs, appropriated for sexual gratification and reproductive labor. The colonial order excludes them from the gaze except as tools for such exploitation, rendering their drives and sensations as extensions of systemic utility rather than sites of agency.

Through dismemberment, the sub-molecular scale enforces a hierarchy of organs and drives, converting intimacy into instruments of control and alienating individuals from their own flesh. Sensory pleasures are no longer shared or mutual; they are extracted, consumed, and redefined to sustain the colonial apparatus.

Molecular Scale: Distorted Bonds and Polarized Relationality

At the molecular scale, desire shifts from dismembered drives to relational dynamics, where bonds between bodies are shaped and manipulated by systems of power. These bonds, rather than fostering mutuality, are distorted into polarized configurations that reinforce hierarchies of domination and subjugation.

WHITE MEN

White men dominate molecular bonds, positioning themselves as sovereign subjects who dictate the terms of relationality. Their interactions with white women emphasize possession and protection, framing the latter as valuable but subordinate. Bonds with colonized men and women are exploitative—reducing men to laboring bodies or casting them as either emasculated subjects or exaggerated threats, while rendering women instruments of sexual and reproductive exploitation.

WHITE WOMEN

White women's relational bonds reflect their dual role as both objects and agents of the white male gaze within the colonial order. Interactions with colonized individuals—particularly men—are often framed as pseudo-transgressive gestures of rebellion against white male authority. Yet, often despite their intentions, these relations reaffirm colonial fantasies of the colonized man as either emasculated subject or hypersexual threat—sustaining and eroticizing this figure for the white male gaze in both overt and insidious ways. Bonds with colonized women similarly reinforce hierarchical structures, as white women appropriate their labor, style, and sensuality to augment their own visibility and desirability within the colonial schema.

COLONIZED MEN

Colonized men experience relationality as a site of hypervisibility and control. Bonds with white women are criminalized and sensationalized, reinforcing narratives of danger, corruption, and sexual transgression. Within colonized communities, these men may internalize colonial hierarchies, attempting to reclaim a masculinity denied by the colonial order through assertions of dominance over colonized women—thus reproducing the very logics of subjugation that disempower them.

COLONIZED WOMEN

Colonized women are marginalized and exploited within relational bonds. Their interactions with white men are defined by coercion and violence in both subtle and spectacular ways, reducing them to casual objects of conquest. Bonds with colonized men are often shaped by the residual effects of colonial domination, where patterns of subjugation and control are replicated. Relations with white women typically erase their agency, treating them as tools or accessories for white women's social and aesthetic empowerment.

At the molecular scale, the colonial order distorts intimacy into mechanisms of control, transforming relational bonds into sites of exploitation and subordination. Mutuality is systematically denied, and relations are restructured to perpetuate the dynamics of possession, dominance, and dispossession.

MOLAR SCALE: CODIFICATION AND SYSTEMIC ABSTRACTION

The molar scale abstracts bodies and relations into systemic categories, embedding the colonial order into institutional frameworks of governance, law, and culture. Through visual and symbolic abstractions, molar systems normalize hierarchies and ensure their reproduction across populations.

WHITE MEN

As architects of systemic frameworks, white men codify their dominance into laws, cultural norms, and administrative structures. These systems position them as protectors of white women and arbiters of colonized bodies, embedding their gaze and authority into the fabric of society.

WHITE WOMEN

White women's roles are institutionalized through systems that reinforce their desirability, purity, and alignment with white male dominance. Legal and cultural narratives privilege their status as possessions of white men while enabling them to wield power over colonized populations, particularly colonized women, through appropriation and exclusion.

Colonized Men

Colonized men are hyper-visible within molar systems, their sexuality and agency criminalized and policed through laws and cultural narratives that depict them as threats to white purity and order. This codification ensures their subjugation while maintaining their utility as laborers or symbols of deviance.

Colonized Women

Colonized women are, again, paradoxically rendered disposable yet indispensable within molar systems, abstracted into reproductive and laboring bodies. Their erasure from institutional frameworks normalizes their exploitation, treating them as resources rather than individuals. This sustains their disposability and ensures their subordination within the colonial hierarchy.

By reducing bodies and relations to functions within a system, the molar scale perpetuates the colonial order through abstraction and codification. Visual and symbolic abstractions—such as anthropometric measurements, racial categories, and legal definitions—transform individuals into populations that can be governed, exploited, and erased.

Social media exemplifies the molar scale's mechanisms of abstraction, surveillance, and commodification. It extends the colonial gaze into digital spaces, breaking down bodies into visual content and reducing relational dynamics into metrics of visibility and validation. For colonized individuals, social media amplifies hyper-visibility and erasure simultaneously, commodifying their aesthetics while erasing their agency. The platformization of relationality reconfigures bonds into performances tailored for an audience governed by the colonial gaze, reproducing hierarchies sedimented by colonial structures and libidinal economies.

The Role of Same-Sex Relations

Same-sex relationships within the colonial order often reflect and sustain its hierarchies of power. Whether involving white and colonized individuals or occurring exclusively within these groups, such relationships frequently reproduce racialized and gendered dynamics, perpetuating the colonial logic of dismemberment, exploitation, and internalized oppression.

White Men and Colonized Men
Same-sex relationships between white men and col-

onized men often involve fetishization, with colonized men reduced to hypersexualized or submissive roles. White men use systemic power to dominate these relationships, framing themselves as active subjects while rendering colonized men consumable objects, as keenly observed by Vincent Woodard in *The Delectable Negro: Human Consumption and Homoeroticism within U.S. Slave Culture* (2014). For colonized men, such dynamics can lead to internalized hierarchies, where exaggerated masculinity or submission becomes a performance to gain validation, ultimately reinforcing colonial power structures.

WHITE WOMEN AND COLONIZED WOMEN

In relationships between white and colonized women, colonized partners are frequently fetishized or treated as tools for the white partner's self-discovery. White women often position these relationships as liberatory while erasing the agency and autonomy of colonized women, reducing them to roles of servility or hypersexuality. These dynamics perpetuate colonial hierarchies by upholding whiteness as the center of desire and validation.

AMONGST WHITES

Same-sex relationships among white men and white women typically consolidate privilege by excluding colonized individuals. White men's relationships often center homosocial bonding that reinforces their dominance, while white women's relationships tend to obscure their complicity in colonial exploitation. Both cases sustain whiteness as the norm, appropriating aspects of colonized cultures without challenging molecular polarities and molar inequalities.

AMONGST THE COLONIZED

Same-sex relationships among colonized men and colonized women are deeply affected by internalized colonial hierarchies. Among men, these relationships may replicate domination and submission, mirroring colonial emasculation and reinforcing cycles of harm. Among men as well as women, dynamics of colorism and proximity to colonial ideals can unravel their entanglements.

Same-sex relationships in the colonial order often sustain its hierarchies, mirroring its dynamics of power and subjugation. These relationships frequently perpetuate objectification, fetishization, and internalized oppression.

The "Talented Tenth"

The "talented tenth" among colonized men and women—particularly Black individuals—often navigates the colonial order's dismemberment of bodies and relations through two seemingly opposed responses, or else by oscillating sharply, even schizophrenically, between them. Some assume the posture of exception, striving for assimilation through respectability politics and distancing themselves from the colonial gaze's fetishization of their racialized features. Others seize hypervisibility, deliberately embodying and amplifying the very traits that gaze desires. Yet both responses, despite their contrast, remain tethered to the same colonial grammar: they preserve the binary structures of control and exploitation by centering the white male gaze as privileged subject, while rendering the "talented tenth" its object—produced to appease, provoke, or gratify.

Exceptions: Policing and Correcting Blackness
The exception-oriented talented tenth reacts to racialized shame by disciplining their bodies and behaviors to project respectability and competence.

On the sub-molecular scale, the exceptions counter stereotypes by controlling their appearance and actions—Black men emphasize refinement, and Black women emphasize competence—concealing internalized shame while redirecting energy toward self-surveillance.

On the molecular scale, the exceptions form alliances with white elites, gaining access to power but fracturing their communities.

On the molar scale, the exceptions embody "success" within colonial systems, legitimizing the hierarchy by appearing to prove advancement is possible through compliance.

While they aim to escape the stigmas attached to their assigned race, their conformity often reinforces the systems that perpetuate it.

Exaggerations: Caricaturing and Fetishizing Blackness

By contrast, others amplify the fetishized traits associated with their assigned race, transforming themselves into spectacles that align with colonial stereotypes.

On the sub-molecular scale, the exaggerations exoticize physical traits and behaviors labeled "primitive", decadent, or dangerous, reinforcing their organs as objects of spectacle.

On the molecular scale, the exaggerations form relationships that center on performing authenticity for validation or attention, perpetuating colonial dynamics of exploitation.

On the molar scale, the exaggerations achieve hypervisibility by leaning into stereotypes—becoming symbols of deviant or excessive Blackness—within systemic frameworks that reward spectacle.

This strategy appears defiant but ultimately confirms the colonial framework, which relies on such extremes to sustain its gaze.

Two Talented Tenths, One Colonial Order

The "talented tenth" illustrates two contrasting strategies for navigating the colonial order. One group seeks to be exceptions, conforming to norms of respectability and discipline to distance themselves from the stigmas imposed on their racialized identity. These individuals sanitize their behaviors, project competence, and leverage relationships with white elites to gain visibility, inadvertently legitimizing the colonial hierarchy by seeming to validate its meritocratic myth.

The other group embodies the colonial gaze, exaggerating traits fetishized by the system—hypersexuality, perceived primitivism, or exaggerated cultural markers. By performing these extremes, they capitalize on hypervisibility, becoming spectacles of Blackness, Native-ness, Asian-ness, or other racialized identities that align with colonial stereotypes. Despite their apparent defiance, this approach also reinforces the colonial framework, one as the disciplined "good subject," the other as the exotic "spectacle."

Together, these dual responses serve the colonial order as complementary tools of control. The sanitized exception reinforces the system's legitimacy by modeling conformity, while the exaggerated embodiment sustains its fetishizing logic. Meanwhile, the vast majority of colonized peoples, who reject alignment with either pole, are left navigating a foresaken middle ground, forced to balance the oppressive demands of these imposed extremes.

REJECTING THE COLONIAL ORDER

The "successes" of the talented tenth within these frameworks underscores the insidious reach of the colonial system. Their complicity reinforces the myth of individual merit, obscuring the structural conditions that necessitate subservience and perpetuate domination. These fractures deepen divisions within colonized communities, undermining the formation of communizing bonds.

Liberation cannot arise from the pursuit of distinction within a system built on oppression. Instead, it demands a rejection of the foundational logics of the colonial order—its polarities, hierarchies, and mechanisms of control. By dismantling these dualities and forging bonds rooted in mutuality rather than visibility or compliance, it becomes possible to resist the systems that sustain domination and erasure. True liberation lies not in achieving success within colonial structures but in imagining and creating worlds beyond their reach.

FUGITIVE EROTICS
Kinship in Resistance and Transformation

Colonial systems sought to dismember enslaved Africans physically, emotionally, and socially, reducing them to tools of labor and domination. Through systemic violence—family separations, cultural erasure, and the commodification of the flesh—these regimes aimed to undermine and destroy autonomy, relationality, and collective resistance. Yet, enslaved Africans resisted this dehumanization by transforming dismemberment into connection, forging profound bonds through practices of (re-)creative repair.

Fred Moten's concept of resistance and (re-)creation "in the break" (2003) helps illuminate how the fractured flesh of enslavement became a site for radical transformative reparations. In this context, displacement gave rise to practices of relationality that were invisible to and beyond the comprehension and control of colonial systems yet radically transformative for those engaged in them. Through acts of (re-)creation—drumming, singing, storytelling, and spirit invocation—what was broken down through violence was reconstituted into fugitive assemblies of intimacy and vitality.

Across the African diaspora, spiritual traditions such as Vodou in Haiti, Candomblé and Umbanda in Brazil, Hoodoo in the United States, Santería in Cuba, and Obeah in the British West Indies embody this (re-)creative practice of transformation. In these practices, seemingly dismembered cosmologies and rituals were reassembled into sacred acts of escape and transformation. By privileging erotic proximity over pornoscopic distance, improvisational fluidity over typographic fixity, and sacred invisibility over commodified hyper-visibility, these traditions offer profound resistance to colonial logics.

Diffracting Africa

The history of the African diaspora is better understood as a story of diffractive warping rather than discretizing rupture. Myths of "de-Africanization" claim that the Middle Passage severed African peoples from their cultural roots, framing Black diasporic traditions as disconnected fragments. However, the forced displacement of African peoples functioned as a diffraction—a scattering and transformation that spread African cosmologies and practices without rendering them discontinuous.

The Door of No Return was not a rupture but an aperture, diffracting African rites and rituals into dynamic, adaptive practices. Far from destroying these traditions, the violence of the Middle Passage revealed their continuities and in-/re-surgencies. This diffraction amplified longstanding cultural entanglements that had been forged over millennia of intra-/inter-action across the continent, transforming them into dynamic practices of survival and resistance. Central organizing principles of African cosmologies—polyrhythms, call-and-response, rituals of possession, and ubuntu oriented, community organizing—traveled through this diffraction apparatus, merging with Indigenous and European influences.

What Amiri Baraka termed the "changing same" of Afro-diasporic traditions demonstrates the transformative force of diffraction, where continuity is not broken but scattered and reshaped. The Egungun masquerades of the Yoruba, which honor ancestral spirits, are kin to Haitian Vodou's Gede spirits, who creatively mend the rupture between life and death through irreverence and laughter. The Kongo cosmogram, a sacred depiction of the crossroads as a site of spiritual convergence and transformation, (re-)encountered the Yoruba orisha of the crossroads, Eshu, and was diffracted into Haitian Vodou's Papa Legba and his associated veve cosmogram. The Ifá divination system, carried by enslaved Yoruba, diffused into the Americas, evolving into Santería's and Candomblé's cowrie shell readings, each adapting to the survival needs of their respective New Worlds, Cuba and Brazil, while retaining the sacred logic of relationality and revelation. These practices collectively illuminate how the spiritual rites of the Niger-Congo linguistic, psychic, and rhythmic continuum traversed continental Africa, endured the Middle Passage, and adapted to displacement, sustaining their transformative force.

Kinship as a Diffraction of Continuity

Kinship among Afro-diasporic traditions emerges from diffraction, creating relational systems that sustain resistance and transformation. These connections can be understood through homological, analogical, and ecological figures, reflecting distinct yet intertwined forms of relationality.

Homological Kinship involves shared origins that diverged in response to local conditions. Just as the bones in a whale's fins and a bat's wings share a common evolutionary origin but have adapted to different environments, traditions like Vodou, Candomblé, and Santería retain core African cosmological structures while transforming to meet the material and spiritual realities of the Americas. For example, the Yoruba *orixás*, reinterpreted as saints in

Santería, illustrate the (re-)creative resilience of African cosmologies as they were adapted to survive Catholic colonial frameworks.

Analogical Kinship arises through convergence, reflecting shared life conditions and responses despite different origins. Similar to the convergent evolution of the snake form in multiple reptilian lineages, Afro-diasporic traditions independently developed analogous practices to address overlapping traumas of displacement and commodification. Spirit possession, for instance, appears in Vodou, Candomblé, and Obeah, offering anologous means of reclaiming agency and intimacy in a world of colonial abstraction. These parallel strategies demonstrate how disparate traditions converge in functionality, resisting oppression through shared creative expressions.

Ecological Kinship emerges through co-evolution and interaction within shared cultural ecosystems. Just as orchids evolve to mimic the pheromones of their pollinators, Afro-diasporic traditions evolved symbiotically with one another and their environments. Haitian Vodou, for instance, mimics elements of Catholicism and Indigenous Taíno spirituality, while Brazilian Candomblé mimics Indigenous rites from the Atlantic and Amazonian rainforests alongside Catholicism. These dynamic interactions create adaptive cultural ecologies, transforming dismemberment into assemblies of (re-)creative repair and relational resilience.

By understanding these kinships, we see how Afro-diasporic traditions channeled (re-)creative practices that resist colonial domination through the breaks of displacement and disconnection. Black rites of breakage and repair involving kindred rhythms, chants, and dances are evidence of in-/re-surgences of Afro-diasporic modes of relationality at every level, from the submolecular to the molar.

Transforming Breakage into Beauty and Sublimity

Afro-diasporic spiritualities embody a transformative philosophy of repair, where acts of recollection and reparation do not seek to preserve the past as it was but instead create something radically new. This philosophy resonates with kintsugi (金継ぎ)—the Japanese art of repairing broken ceramics with gold to emphasize both their breakage and repair—and its more extreme counterpart, yobitsugi (呼び継ぎ). Yobitsugi gathers fragments from different vessels to create a wholly new and original form, embracing differences and imperfections. This openness to creolization parallels Afro-diasporic traditions, which turn the fractures of history into sites of diffraction, regarding them as apertures rather than ruptures.

As Derek Walcott observed, "Break a vase, and the love that reassembles the fragments is stronger than that love which took its symmetry for granted when it was whole." This ethos lies at the heart of fugitive erotics, a practice central to Afro-diasporic traditions. The act of repair is not an attempt to erase the breaks of history but to honor them, reassembling breaks into wholes that carry new meaning. Much like the Caribbean art Walcott describes, which gathers shards of history, culture, and language into creolized expressions, Afro-diasporic spiritualities writ large transform the shattered legacies of colonial violence into openings for vitality and (re-)creativity.

Viewed through the lens of yobitsugi, these traditions remind us that fragility is inevitable; breaks may reoccur through accident, negligence, or cruel design. Yet resilience lies in the ongoing practice of repair itself, not in any promise of permanence and wholeness beyond breakage. Through rituals of invisibility, embodiment, and ineffability, Afro-diasporic spiritualities reclaim relationality as beauty and sublimity in the break. Invisibility shields the flesh from colonial surveillance, ineffability resists reduction to abstraction, and (re-)embodiment repairs broken bonds of intimacy. Together, these practices turn dismemberment into flourishing.

Afro-diasporic spiritualities offer a forceful counter-narrative to colonial dismemberment, demonstrating how broke down bodies and displaced communities generate new forms of intimacy, kinship, and liberation. Traditions like Vodou, Candomblé, Obeah, Santería, and Hoodoo weave together homological, analogical, and ecological kinships that transform displacement into (re-)creative resilience. These practices assert that the dismembered is not broken but (re-)creatively remembered, offering a profound testament to the enduring power of creativity, connection, and collective renewal. Like yobitsugi, they render ruptures of history into apertures for sublimity and possibility, reminding us that even in the face of violence, transformation and repair remain vital forces.

Sub-Molecular Fugitivity: Becoming(s) Invisible

At the sub-molecular scale, colonial systems reduced the body to dismembered organs and drives, rendering its fleshy organs hyper-visible and exploitable as tools for labor, reproduction, or fetishization. This pornoscopic dismemberment stripped the flesh of vitality, agency, and sacredness, commodifying it into an object of domination. Afro-diasporic spiritualities counter this reduction by reclaiming the flesh as a site where the unseen unfolds—a dynamic and living field of potential where drives converge and diverge unpredictably. Through ritual, embodied practice, and the invocation of invisible forces, the flesh is reconstituted as a vessel of vitality, repair, and resistance.

In Vodou, the flesh becomes a portal for spirits such as the Gede, who defy colonial reduction through irreverence, laughter, and the erotic forces of death and regeneration. Possession rituals exemplify how the rupture of the flesh is reclaimed as an aperture for channeling invisible forces and enacting sacred transformations. When a devotee is "mounted" by a spirit, their flesh is animated by something beyond the hyper-visibility of colonial categorization, becoming a conduit for unseen forces—ancestors, deities, and energies that resist commodification. This alignment of flesh and spirit affirms that the flesh is always more than meets the eye: inhabited by something beyond colonial surveillance and control.

Herbal practices in Hoodoo and Obeah transform the flesh's sub-molecular dismemberment into sites of (re-)creative repair and renewal. The ritual use of plants, charged with spiritual intent, channels unseen forces to counteract physical and spiritual ailments inflicted by colonial violence. Rootworkers combine botanical knowledge with spiritual invocations of invisible forces, crafting healing balms, protective charms, and revitalizing tinctures. These practices prioritize the felt over the seen, reclaiming the sacred connection between human and non-human others through relationships with forces that elude visualization.

Through rhythmic drumming, chanting, and possession, Afro-diasporic traditions align dismembered drives into fleeting but profound coherence. Drums act as "cosmic heartbeats," generating resonances that connect participants to ancestral energies and disrupt colonial dismemberment. Possession of the flesh exemplifies sub-molecular fugitivity, where the seen and unseen intertwine, transforming hyper-visible fragments into conduits for invisible forces of resistance.

MOLECULAR FUGITIVITY: INTIMACY IN THE BREAK

At the molecular scale, colonial systems distorted relational bonds, replacing communizing mutualities with polarizing hierarchies. Enslaved individuals were denied the ability to form reciprocal connections, as their organs or "means of relation" were recast as tools for appropriation and exploitation. Afro-diasporic spiritualities counter this distortion by cultivating communizing bonds—forging fugitive assemblies alloyed through shared presence, mutual sensing, and rites of breakage and repair.

In Vodou ceremonies, circular dances around the *poto mitan* (central pillar) embody relational intimacy, synchronizing participants with shared rhythms and movements that dissolve boundaries between the individual, the community, and the divine. These dances resonate with Yoruba *oríkì* traditions, where praise songs forge intimacy between humans and *orixás*, and with the call-and-response structure of Black gospel music, which builds relationality through collective improvisation. Fugitive erotics at this scale celebrates these moments as acts of mutual aid, where collective rhythms resist alienation.

Possession rituals further demonstrate molecular fugitivity by dissolving hierarchies of power and centering shared presence. When spirits such as Ogun or Erzulie possess a devotee, they bring divine intimacy into the community, allowing the collective to experience relationality as a dynamic interplay between seen and unseen forces. In Candomblé, the *terreiro* serves as a space where devotees honor their *orixás* through music, dance, and offerings, fostering a web of mutual aid that sustains the community against external pressures. These spaces cultivate fugitive erotics by prioritizing the collective over the individual, forging communizing bonds that defy colonial dismemberment and polarization.

By embracing relationality "in the break," these practices transform colonial distortions into confluent and co-constituted bonds. Shared rhythms, movements, and invocations reassemble broken flesh to form communizing bonds between bodies, reclaiming intimacy as a site of resistance and flourishing.

Molar Fugitivity: Becoming(s) Ineffable

At the molar scale, colonial systems imposed abstraction, reducing individuals to populations, bodies to exploitable categories, and intimacy to tools of control. These abstractions flattened complexity, enforced systemic domination, and sought to consolidate power into centralized, totalizing structures. Afro-diasporic spiritualities resist these molar systems by privileging ineffable forces—connections and truths that evade codification and reduction. In doing so, these rites ward off the formation of molar administrations within their communities, operating in a manner reminiscent of Pierre Clastres' *Societies Against the State* (1974).

Clastres identifies how so-called "primitive" societies resist centralized authority by ensuring that power remains distributed and non-coercive. Similarly, Afro-diasporic practices maintain their dynamic, decentralized nature, resisting the consolidation of power into hierarchical structures. For instance, in Santería, the orishas embody ineffability through their dynamic, multifaceted identities. Eleguá, the guardian of crossroads, defies fixed representation by embodying opposites—creation and destruction, youth and age, playfulness and wisdom—in "tricky" and "wicked" ways. The rituals that summon Eleguá, particularly through drumming, evade transcription or replication outside of their embodied contexts. This ineffability resists abstraction, ensuring that no single entity or institution can monopolize or dictate spiritual authority.

In Haitian Vodou, rituals for the Gede spirits incorporate humor, bawdiness, and irreverence, rejecting the solemnity that often characterizes hierarchical systems of control. These acts undermine the rigidity of colonial frameworks, asserting vitality and improvisation in the face of systemic oppression. Similarly, Hoodoo's rootwork remains profoundly singular and situational, adapting spells and potions to meet specific circumstances. This improvisational flexibility prevents the ossification of practices into rigid, codified systems, preserving autonomy and dynamism within the tradition.

These practices operate as what Clastres describes as "the ruse of culture against power," ensuring that leadership and authority remain humble, diffuse, and controlled by communal participation rather than centralized coercion. Like the chief in Clastres' analysis, spiritual leaders in Afro-diasporic traditions derive their authority from the collective rather than imposing it. They rely on charisma, knowledge, and the ability to foster relationality, rather than coercive power, to guide rituals and maintain communal harmony. This distributed structure, which keeps power subordinate to the collective, echoes Clastres' assertion that "culture uses against power the very ruse of nature."

By privileging oral transmission, embodied presence, and sensory practices, Afro-diasporic spiritualities resist the abstractions that facilitate totalizing control. These practices ensure that power remains diffuse and relational, warding off the formation of rigid hierarchies or centralized administrations. Like Clastres' societies against the state, Afro-diasporic rites of breakage and repair transform the exercise of power into a collective, participatory process, creating spaces where intimacy and relationality thrive, and systemic domination is continuously thwarted.

In doing so, they assert a forceful counter-narrative to colonial systems of abstraction, offering models of resistance and resilience rooted in improvisation and call-and-response.

ALL FUGITIVE EROTICS ARE QUEER

Fugitive erotics transforms the colonial break into a site of reimagined intimacy and connection. At its heart lies a refusal of the colonial order of sexuality—a system that fragments bodies, distorts relational bonds, and codifies hierarchies of domination. This refusal finds its fullest expression in queer transitions, becomings that unsettle fixed categories of gender, sexuality, and embodiment.

In contrast, proper transitions often reflect a desire to inhabit, rather than dismantle, the colonial order. Certain white trans men transition to wield the colonial gaze, moving from object to subject in pursuit of the privileges of white cis masculinity—control, authority, and dominance. Conversely, certain white trans women transition to embody the prize object of that same gaze, aligning themselves with ideals of white cis femininity to evade the "responsibility" that comes with wielding authority and control. While these transitions reject assigned sex, they often reproduce the colonial hierarchies of gender and power. Emerging from a sense of misplacement within the system, proper transitions ultimately reaffirm its binaries, logics, and structures of possession.

Queer transitions, by contrast, refuse containment and the pursuit of legibility within colonial frameworks. They embrace confluences, multiplicities, and relationality, unsettling fixed boundaries of identity and becoming otherwise. Afro-diasporic spiritual traditions—such as Haitian Vodou, Cuban Santería, and Brazilian Candomblé—embody this refusal. As Roberto Strongman argues in *Queering Black Atlantic Religions* (2019), these traditions treat the body as an open vessel through rituals of trance/trans possession, where gender and identity are not fixed but emerge as relational, spiritual, and distinct from biological sex.

To say all fugitive erotics are queer is to name their refusal of fixity, their embrace of movement, and their transformation of rupture into aperture. Queer transitions, unlike proper transitions, do not strive to achieve placement within the colonial order but instead dissolve its boundaries altogether. They reconstitute the break as a site of fluidity and creation, where bodies, relations, and desires become conduits for unseen forces of repair, vitality, and liberation. In this way, queer transitions affirm the sacred potential of becoming otherwise—of refusing the colonial gaze and imagining worlds beyond its reach.

Erotic Proximity in the Break

Fugitive erotics transforms the colonial "break" into a site of erotic proximity, reclaiming intimacy and relationality as forces of liberation. Afro-diasporic spiritualities operate on multiple levels to persist and resist in spite of dismemberment and abstraction.

- Sub-Molecular: Restoring the flesh's sacred vitality through invisibility, shielding it from colonial surveillance and making it a site of unseen potential.
- Molecular: Reconfiguring distorted bonds into dynamic assemblies of mutual aid and collective presence, centering intimacy in shared rhythms, movements, and invocations.
- Molar: Resisting visual and symbolic abstraction by privileging ineffable connections that evade categorization and nurture relationality as a dynamic and sacred practice.

Through homological, analogical, and ecological kinship, Afro-diasporic traditions evince the enduring creativity of Black life in the break. From the invocation of *orixás* in Candomblé to the humor of the Gede in Vodou and the improvisational spells of Hoodoo, these practices redefine intimacy and desire across scales as forces of connection, vitality, and liberation.

Centering erotic proximity and rejecting pornoscopic distance, fugitive erotics is the force of Afro-diasporic spiritualities to transform breakage into beauty and sublimity. Through rituals of (re-)embodiment, invisibility, and ineffability, these traditions reclaim relationality as a site of collective resistance and sacred renewal, offering profound models for (de-/re-)constructing worlds beyond systems of domination.

THE BREAK: CHICAGO HOUSE
A Panel at BADS_lab (Black Arts & Decolonial Sciences)

Thanks to drum machines, sound systems, and repurposed warehouses and basements, 1980s Chicago House Music opened up a future that was Black, brown, and queer. DJs invented new ways of marking and keeping time within community. In the years since, computation has made music-making more accessible. What kinds of collectivities are still to come?

Combining complementary modes of thinking, making, and performing, *Futurhythmachines: House* (FRM:*House*) was a daylong public event held on May 11, 2024. Organized during the BADS_lab, it featured a DIY synthesizer workshop, a panel discussion, and a DIY synth performance with a reception.

BADS_lab director Muindi Fanuel Muindi (philosopher and poet) moderated a panel with Dr. Thomas DeFrantz (Black social dance historian and technology theorist), DJ Duane Powell (House DJ and music historian), and Meida McNeal (multi-disciplinary performance artist and critical ethnographer). They discussed the sonic and social architectures of Chicago House and its surrounds. The panel placed Chicago House within a long lineage of antiphonal experiments in the Black Arts, which have gathered people in movement and in apposition to prevailing paradigms of capture, control, and containment.

MEIDA:

Chicago house music. To me, it is a culture. It is, in some sense, our folk culture. I think it's about community, creativity, and innovation.

DUANE:

Chicago has always been known—especially within my community—for its segregation. Not just segregation by race, but by neighborhoods. People didn't really leave their neighborhoods, but house music was the one thing that, for my generation and my people, desegregated us because we followed it. We went all over the city, following this music and culture. For me, I literally grew up in Roseland on 116th Street, but I was hanging out at Medusas up on Belmont, or in Maywood, traveling by train in the wee hours of the morning, following the music.

In doing so, house also awakened me to the idea of travel. I feel like house music, even when I was here, made me more of a global citizen, just following where the music was going. And that's kind of been a part of my practice ever since.

TOMMY:

For me, house is a scaffolding logic that encourages us to wonder beyond.

I'm thinking about how house has to get squashed to fit on radio because radio doesn't want to take time, but house tends to want time to operate really differently, to become expansive. Disco couldn't figure that out. Funk did that, though, too. Funk and house are very similar in a certain way.

But then, if we look at funk and house, maybe we can think about a kind of masculinist and femme space. House, for me, is definitely something that I could argue as a femme queer space that we so desperately need. So, when it comes forward, it creates a space that needed to be there, that perhaps wasn't there before. And in relationship to HIV, AIDS, and things that are happening on the planet...

MEIDA:

Most folks who were in the original generations of house, I think we were kind of apprenticed in—brought in by family, by cousins, by someone else who brought you into the culture.

So, thinking about that as a kind of lineage, right? And teasing that out, then thinking about the spaces where women—yes, women—played in house, and thinking a lot about vocalists, but then also some of the DJs who emerged. We began to think about house in the context of the Great Migration and Black folks coming here in waves from 1910 through the 1970s, from the South to the North. First, on the South Side, in the Black Belt, a contained area, then to the West Side. Each of those waves was bringing Black social culture into this space, and then transforming it—jazz, blues, and so on. House comes out of that, right?

Again, so many DJs and other folks in the culture have family or folks who had, like, a bar, a lounge, or a club in the neighborhood, and those were some of the first places they heard music, heard records spun. When we get to what is properly known as house in the '80s, there's still this connection to funk, to disco—those influences don't go away. Those are the influences that created the first records. Those are the sounds that Vince Lawrence and Jesse Saunders were thinking about when they started to make beats, you know?

DUANE:

Yeah. I mean, because I'm thinking about, you know, in the days when the culture was formed. So, whenever we talk about house, we always have to remember that there's house the culture, and there's house the genre. The culture inspired the genre, and the culture was really formed years before even disco was a thing, in the early '70s, just after the Civil Rights Movement. You know, what we thought we were going to get from the promises of the Civil Rights Movement, right?

Chicago was the first city to have a version of a gay rights organization. Illinois was the first state to decriminalize certain acts of homosexuality. But what Chicago still had was a segregation issue. A lot of the clubs and places at the time, like one called Dugan's Bistro, had a quota. They wouldn't allow a certain number of Black people into the space, and they would overcard them, just things of that nature, which sparked these guys to go and create spaces for themselves. Those spaces ended up being these parties at these houses in South Shore.

The first time the term "house" comes into play wasn't the Warehouse; it was the parties thrown at these houses in South Shore. So, that has me thinking about a couple of things: about needing space, and these guys needing space to be themselves.

I had to do a talk one time at the Stoney Island Arts Bank because they had just acquired the gazebo for Tamir Rice, who was killed in Cleveland, and they wanted to do some talks around it. They wanted to somehow connect the Tamir Rice gazebo with the other collections they had at the bank. And with me being the steward of the Frankie Knuckles collection, I had to do a talk linking the Tamir Rice gazebo to the Frankie Knuckles record collection. It's like, "Okay, how am I supposed to do this?"

Then I was introduced to an article that was written by Dr. Wallace Best around that time. I want to say it was about either Tamir Rice or Eric Garner or someone's killing. He had a quote that hit me like a lightbulb. He said, "With all of those killings, the police killings, what was this person's first crime? They moved." And it started to make me think about those times when people like Craig and others were being policed at Dugan's Bistro and elsewhere, anytime they did anything. How our movement was a threat, how movement was policed, and how we needed these spaces where we could be and then move freely without being regarded as a threat

TOMMY:

Okay, I was thinking about... Well, because I know you're recording, right? Should I do this in my white voice.... I was thinking about, you know, this rhetoric of freedom, which is really important to how Black people understand culture to be organized. At the same time, we're really good with contradiction. Black life is full of contradiction. We're very good at it. So, we can be all about the Roland 808, but anti-capitalist at the same time and outside of commerce. Like... We're amazing.

So, this idea that there's freedom, but there's also genre—like, you're free to move inside of house any way you want. But are you really? Not really. You can't really do just anything at the same time. Yet we know that the dance, the form, the culture wants to be free and open, and that contradiction, I just think, is really important to thinking about how Black culture organizes itself, and how we look and how we move, to your point.

So, our movements offer us this kind of ancestor worship in the gesture, even if somebody else can't understand that. So, the movement can do the thing without seeming to do the thing, and it can also undo the thing.

I think about that in your work so much, Meida—how the work of Honey Pot undoes expectations, or regulations, or normativities by making something else that didn't seem to be there before, but was there all along. I feel like that's what house did, or continues to do, from my little point of view. It's a different point of view, of course.

I'm curious about putting it near disco. Disco, of course, was usually live and whatnot. So, then this idea that it does a certain thing—maybe they're doing things in different venues, instead of against each other. Do you think that's fair?

DUANE:

I'm just going, "Yes!" I mean, I feel like disco is in conversation with house here in this city. You know, people will often conflate the two. But I think part of that is embracing this kind of freedom or pushing against, you know, "when we come in here, we can free up, we can imagine ourselves other, to be prepared to go back out and deal with that stuff." I think that ethos bridges from disco to house.

I also think that Chicago is a center where, like, R&B and soul—a certain sound—came out of here, and records were produced. There were labels, until that went away and got shut down by capitalism, eaten up, you know? But that legacy of sound, and that respect for music, I think, continues to go through disco and then comes into house for so many in the culture. But even when they say disco, I've often pushed back against this idea that house rose from the ashes of disco's demolition. It's false, you know, because a lot of the music that inspired house really wasn't disco. It was just like 10%, right, because of that social lineage.

I mean, think about Vince Lawrence and them—they all came from a musical legacy, some of which was directly tied to people like Curtis Mayfield. So, it was just soulful energy. And house has never been about the drum pattern, 4/4 and whatever. It's about the groove, and it's why we've been able to extract it from anywhere and everywhere—in terms of disco, jazz, funk, absolutely. You know, all forms of electronic music, we've been able to extract from, because it's all about the soul of it.

Yeah, I think that's also where the respect for blending comes in. Like, if you can't blend right, if you can't blend, then you—! To the point that scared me, that kept me away from using it for a long time, because it's like, if your blends aren't tight, if you're not blending these sounds, you're going to get raked over the coals. Yes. And I was like, I'm not ready.

MUINDI:

One thing which I think all of you also observed, is that house was birthed in spaces where all these different types of music were being played—blends of rhythm and blues, soul and funk. One thing to add is that many of the electronic musical instruments in circulation at the time immediately prior to house's inception weren't being used to create "finished" recordings by those Chicago recording studios that first purchased them. Instead, you know, if somebody wanted to create the skeleton of a track, or wanted to give someone an idea or a sketch for a track, electronic musical instruments were more often used for creating skeletons and producing sketches and filling in gaps when you couldn't find a live musician.

Chicago had a bunch of record studios where all of these machines were being used, and then suddenly these record studios closed, and these things were in pawn shops. People were like, "Oh, I'll buy that drum machine," and then they started blending electronic beats into their sets to get people to keep up the energy, the pace, and the vibe of the dancing "in the break(s)" between different disco and funk tracks. It was like, "Ooh, I can insert a little something like this here." And house as a genre kind of emerges from that desire to produce movement "in the break" being progressively extended and intensified over time, until the dancebreak takes over.

TOMMY:

We need to better understand these new technologies as they come into play. We need to know what these functions are and how they help our practice. We need to stop talking about your work, Duane, as being that of a DJ. I was just thinking about being a "spiritual technologist." What is the motivating aesthetic of the work as a DJ? You've offered it as being able to bring the group into the space, or into the community, and I was just thinking about being an electronic spiritual leader in a way—being able to not just know which songs to play. It's more than that. It's a calling towards an understanding of possibility through groove. I was thinking about that, about being a technologist who works in groove, and how that's really interesting. Is that how you think of it?

DUANE:

So that definitely is, and that's why I have an event called "Sunday Service," and that's actually where the idea came from. Because, I don't know, in house music, unlike a lot of other events, we don't really pre-program our sets. We don't really have an idea of where we're going to take this. And there's not a lot—I've never understood for a long time why people want to watch house music these days because we're not fun to watch. We're not doing a lot of technical back-and-forth. We're not scratching. We're not doing all of this. We literally [*gestures the turning of a knob*] and then we have to have the song in long form because it has to feel... it has to, you know? This is why I kind of don't like where we are now, in certain situations, where DJs and promoters think they get more bang for their buck by adding more detail to a bill, and it doesn't allow the DJ to really build a set and work how they work. Because in house culture, especially with the underground, with Frankie and Ron Hardy, the reason why they had such a following was because they had these houses they could be in every week, building their community and their thing, playing for six hours, and they could take you on this journey. Whereas, when you're only playing for an hour, you've got to hit it and quit it. You've got to get in and out, and you don't really get a chance to become one with the audience. For me, it has to be a certain point, and then it just builds up. That buildup comes as you explore, and the more the audience is like, "Oh!" You know what I mean? This is a different dynamic."

TOMMY:

So, yeah, that was helpful. I was thinking again about this thing I started with about time. We're trying to think about time somehow. And you know, we have so many ritual services, like the feasts in Trinidad and Jamaica—it's like, when you're going into spirit for six or seven hours...

Then, there's the kind of way that we have these dance forms that are totally tied up with capital, like, I don't know, funky chicken, Renegade, or even Dougie, or something like this, where the dances show up to kind of cause this flash, but they're there to be super temporary.

And house, as a genre, is there, as you're saying, like, to serve time in a different way, maybe. And we just have all of these traditions. We have a really deep history of traditions that evade linear time, or work time, or capital time—like, you're going to be in the place for six or seven hours. You can't be worried about tomorrow. You can't worry about, "I have to go to work," or not. You have to find a way to be in the thing while the thing is happening, and because you're there in the thing happening, that's what makes it possible for it to be so.

I'm just taking your point about needing to build audience or build community and build through time, to resist time as being so urgent in house. And that's really different from other forms of Black stories, like tap dance. You can't be a tap dancer for six hours. Try, but usually, you know, three minutes, and you've shown everything you really have to do, like Bojangles and whatnot. And now people maybe even do two-minute performances, just showing the thing that you want to share, and then it's just a shorter form of expression. I just wanted to say that to lift up how we have all kinds of different modes of physical gesture and expression. It's not just one thing, but how maybe I'm still thinking about it in terms of time and an opening of time towards something else.

MEIDA:

Yeah, that's something that I feel like I have. It's a theme that I keep running into when I talk about house with younger people. A lot of them mourn experiences they have never had and don't know if they'll ever get to have it. There is this sense that, like, we grew up in a moment in which there was a flowering of social spaces and that things weren't as tightly regulated yet. So, you know, dance music, house, was happening in clubs and discos, but it was also in juice bars and in other small spaces in Catholic schools, in sock hops, in public schools, you know. And so you had this range of spaces—in banquet halls, for example—where it was often young people who were throwing these parties. Like, they were business people. They were entrepreneurs as young people, right? But then, by the '90s, the city starts to shut all that down. And then people are chasing parties because they're itinerant. They pop up in a place, and then they're there for a little while, and then they're gone, you know, because they get shut down. And then I think the city just hasn't recovered from that. So we've seen generations of young people come after that who don't have this as part of their history, you know, or experience.

DUANE:

We never recovered from that because, like, the bling era of hip hop started to come in, and that's what changed the landscape of all the nightlife. It was like, again, capitalism came in the same way that I feel like Studio 54 did with disco. The need for you to buy expensive bottles of alcohol and all these other things is really what changed the landscape of nightlife.

It's like she said. Like, my introduction was partying at Catholic schools, all the Catholic schools on the South and West Side in the early '80s through parties. And those parties actually started at Mundelein High School in '75, and those arrangements were made because Catholic schools, like white flight had, you know, they were under-enrolled, right? And so it was a way to bring in some money, some cash for parties, and the money from those parties kept the schools open.

So my first time hearing Frankie Knuckles was at that high school because of our age. We couldn't—we were too young to go to the original Warehouse and Power Plant. And so Kurt Townsend, who was throwing those parties, brought them to us. I first heard a lot of these DJs there. And then, you know, the Lewis brothers had the idea to start renting out ballroom rooms in hotels downtown. And then that's why it's downtown. You know, 14- and 15-year-olds, so you have 300 15-year-olds, and, you know, at the hotel, like the Continental, kind of, you know, following this music.

But then the '90s came. Mayor Daley came in. We had the rave laws that came in. We also had the Bulls begin their winning dynasty. We had Harpo Studios come on with this tourist thing. And so they just tried to clear all of that away to make everything about tourism and capitalism. Slowly but surely, like, our scene just couldn't thrive. The Power Plant closed because they enforced a 2 a.m. license on them, whereas the Power Plant didn't get jumping until 2 a.m. I mean, yeah.

So, again, my generation, at this point, a lot of us were going off to college. A lot of those people who were heavily involved at the time, like we all did, a lot of people left. So there was like a small gap where we were chasing parties, finding ourselves at raves and things of that nature. That wasn't necessarily playing, quote unquote, house, but we still needed space. We still needed somewhere to be, and we didn't really see a river. We haven't, like, I'm seeing now a lot happen. We figured out how to just make space in different places.

TOMMY:

So we've been giving a lot of hints throughout, which is how Black people do. The hints are all in there. It's like this is Spirit work. You can't just drop into it unless you're ready to be a spirit. This is femwork. You can't drop into it if it's about you in an authoritarian, patriarchal, "look at me" way. It's not that. It's community work. We've been saying that from the beginning—it's the work of the group, not of the individual. It's the work of repurposing the machine.

The 808 came up before Roland was trying to make money. Black people made house music with these machines to do something different. And even this idea that they were in pawn shops—like, we found the machines and made them do what we needed them to do. The clues are all in there. It's Black because it's about making a way where there is no way, but also believing in art as the source code of life, and its source code.

So if we want to understand how to survive this day and move to the next, we dance house. If we want to understand how to care for our nieces and nephews we've never met, we dance house. If we want to understand how to build a community that can resist the politics that would say we shouldn't be here, we dance house. We're going to find a place to do it. I love that the Catholic school becomes an underground venue. I just love that. And I want to say thank you for that revelation.

MEIDA:
I think, you know, just the further study and understanding of house as kind of like a philosophy, a set of principles, a way of living, you know, there is so much complexity within it, and so much history. It is the Black diaspora, right? And it is cosmopolitan while it sits in a very specific space and time and local-

ity of Chicago. It is all of that still. And I think sometimes we just think of it as like "four to the floor" music, but it has all of that. To be able to unpack that seriously, I also think that archiving house is urgent. People are passing on, and we need to document their stories. We need people to understand that the mundane, everyday things they have in their homes are part of the stories. When we put them all together, they create a rich tapestry and a complex story of how these things came to be.

So I think that is part of what house is and where it should be going: looking to the future while really caretaking and stewarding the past to understand where we're going. And then I also just think there are amazing young people. I'm so inspired. Duane is a mentor to some of them, you know, who are on the scene. I think it's really important to find ways to lift them up and push them forward in the scene.

TOMMY:

It's a challenge, we tend to generationally make a thing that didn't exist in the same way and then move on to the next. So our impulse to archive is so important. We're all historians here, thinking about histories while participating in the culture we love.

At the same time, the culture keeps moving. It moves towards what's next, but still respects what came before in its own way. The older things have a different kind of place in the limelight, on stage, or in the shining moment. It's challenging because, yes, we love house and know it's not going to go away. The media finds its niche, does its thing, and keeps doing it. At the same time, there will be other forms of music that aren't house. They'll be something else. We need to inspire young people to think beyond that too.

And I guess that's the contradiction. One that is also felt in a different way with respect to how we work with new technology. We were talking about Hammond organs and Roland 808s. We weren't their shareholders, we weren't making money off of saying Roland or Hammond. Yet, we're like, "Yeah, that's my jam. That's my machine."

DUANE:

The first sound system associated with warehouse culture was the Richard Long sound system, which Robert Williams commissioned when he opened the warehouse. He was thinking about the Loft in New York, and Richard Long is the one who built the sound system. Robert Williams called over to New York to convince Richard Long to set up a sound system here because, in house, especially in those spaces, the subs and tweeters all had to be separated. It all mattered because there were a lot of things that jocks would do in house when they were grooving to get the crowd in. The dropping of the bass, for example—nothing but tweeters going, and when you bring that bass back in, the crowd would lose their mind. All of that happens on those separated channels.

That's where the sounds of house began in terms of the club scene. It's very essential, and you definitely know when you're in a space that doesn't have an adequate system for house. House is not about just hearing the music; it's about feeling it. If you don't feel it vibrating within you, the system isn't working right. You can't just put two fifteens on some sticks and think that's going to make the party work. No. It has to be set up properly. Depending on the room, you need a four-point system for the speaker system. It has to be pointed in one direction—the floor. And that floor is sacred.

For us, there's a ceremony that happens in house. We get there, there's hugging, and all of that. But we know, once we hit that area, that's the floor. No drinks, nothing to disrupt that. That four-point system is designed for that, almost like a seance. That's what happens in between it.

So, is this history of the formation and development of these technical systems archived? Yes, that's part of what Meida's work with the *Chicago Black Social Cultural Map* is doing—not just documenting the clubs and lounges, but also the electronic stores where we bought the equipment, the after-hours diners where we would eat. All of that is part of the culture.

For instance, the 95th Street Red Line train station is crucial. A lot of us would converge there because it was the final stop before catching the various buses on the south side. So we all had to meet at 95th, and that's how we met new friends. All of these little things need to be documented.

We also need more documentation about the sound systems and the brands. As time goes on, it's important to understand the evolution of this equipment. From the early days of the Technics 1200s to the CDJs—8s, 2000s, 3000s, and the XDJ systems we have now—each piece of equipment plays a role. We need better understanding and documentation of this because the equipment matters in the scheme of things.

There are certain DJs who won't perform without a specific Bozak mixer. Without it, they're not doing it. For them, it's all about the warmer sound, the rotary versus the slide pitch. The level of control you can have when bringing the sound into the room is part of what makes it different.

MEIDA:

I guess I'll just say that we've actually been trying to move that into our programming. We typically do four programs a year because we find a theme, figure out who's going to be on the panel, record them, transcribe them, then code them, and try to get them back on the online map. So it's a lot of care to make sure that we record the conversation, but also have it in other forms, so we can come back to it. One of the things we've been thinking about is having more conversations. Like in the class I just taught. I had a couple DJs come in. They set up, brought in records, and talked about their entry into the craft, how their tools changed over time, how their sets in various spaces changed over time, and discussed what those practices actually were.

We want to get more into how people have done the thing, how they've learned to do it, and where their craft has gone over time. We'd like to do this within the space of a program so we can see some of that history and what people have learned.

In a larger sense, with the map, as Duane said, the map is built to be about more than just discos, clubs, and juice bars—it also includes retail, food, after-hours spots, and all these things that are part of that new world.

DUANE:

Like fashion. Certain styles are synonymous with hip hop culture, for example, and in its inception, house had its looks. When people saw us, they'd say, "Oh, you one them house models." That's what they would call us, because there was an aesthetic that went with it.

Our meeting places were important too, because a lot of times we were also targets. I remember getting chased by gangs on the West Side coming from a party because our looks made us stand out. We were weirdos. We were the early club kids. So, these meeting spots, like the Marshall Fields clock downtown, or 95th Street, were also places we had to think about as safe spaces where we could meet to get to the other places and take part in the culture.

TOMMY:

We do need to do better at documenting the dance part of it too. Actually, I'm working on this large project about Black social dances, which is going in a lot of directions. It's going to take a number of years to figure out what it is, but one of the things I'm really curious about is how we decide we can dance. Not whether we're good dancers, but how do we practice?

What's interesting about house is that it's such an open forum—a mesh of possibilities. So there's not a lot of instruction on how to dance, and I'm sure your map does this, but how did you figure out how you wanted to dance? You can do that on the floor, in the "seance," if you will, in the space. But we tend to like to know a little more than that. You don't just show up and give it a go and see what's going to happen.

House is very interesting because, unlike the commercial dances I mentioned before, those dances can be practiced with a friend or at home. But house isn't constructed like that. Even in hip hop, floor work, or B-girling, when you're doing breaking and going down to the floor, you have to practice. You can't just get in the cipher and hope for the best. In Chicago, it's basic vocabulary, right? There's a central movement in house, and that's "jacking." The down motion into the floor and the upper body movement—this is the central movement. You see many variations on that, where it might be lower, and people are connected and moving together.

DUANE:

It's funny because, speaking to someone who was a former dancer at that time—obviously, the dance crews and everything else—none of this was actually practiced in house. We didn't even realize we were doing tribal things that were encoded into us, like DNA. We didn't even know. When we got together, we never really called ourselves a "dance crew" because we didn't get together to dance. We just happened to find each other, and we were our community.

The dancing didn't happen until we got to the party. There were no rehearsals. There was no, "Are we all wearing this?" It wasn't like that. When I started hearing about it being like a tribal thing, I remember seeing footage of an African tribe, and I was like, "Wait a minute, they look like us at 2210!" But we had no idea it was just tribal. It's weird, but it's in there. I'm with you.

TOMMY:

This reminds me of the famous story from Malcolm X's autobiography. He says he went to a party, had never danced before, but suddenly he just could dance. That's not really how it works, but at the same time, there are so many things that happen in our lives that we're not aware of. One of the reasons Black people are so interested in art-making is because we've been surrounded by art-making since before we were born. We're surrounded by song, movement, gesture, spoken word, light, fashion, and cooking. These things are so important to who we are because so many things were taken from us. These are the things we have—our intangible heritages.

The idea that you felt it because it was available to you, even without consciously knowing what it was—well, that just makes sense. Do you see what I'm trying to say? It's not like we actually think about these things.

DUANE:

For me, I guess, much as I would say my first introduction to culture was at Catholic school, when I really think about it, I think about growing up as a kid and how my grandmother's house turned into a club.

My grandmother had this house, and the basement had a big paneling in the walls, and my uncles were DJs. I would see my parents, aunts, uncles, and their friends on a regular basis, just after work. But on this particular night, they would get dressed, dressed to the nines. I'd ask, "Where are you going?" and they'd say, "Grandma's basement." All of a sudden, the lights would change. They'd put different color lights in, and the atmosphere would turn into something else. They'd make us go to bed while they would turn the basement into this space.

That was my first time seeing these same people I saw every day, all of a sudden in a social setting centered around the music and fellowship. It was something I hadn't seen before.

In keeping with that, you know, we came up in a time before cell phones, and we had those spaces where the music could vibrate for our bodies. The younger generation came up in a time when music was mostly experienced through hearing, not feeling. I remember one incident that led to me naming my events "Sunday Service." A person came to this party who had never really been to house parties before. She had been to a few, but mostly she would stand back and watch. This particular time, I was playing a song—and I remember the song—because it hit her in a way that it had never hit her before. She lost it. Literally, she lost it, like they say in church—she caught the Holy Ghost.

She was overcome and had to be taken off the floor. Later, she came to me, embarrassed. I told her, "Welcome. Back in the day, that's what the music did to us." I hadn't seen that happen in a long time, so I was actually glad. No one pulled out their phones and recorded her. They let her have her moment. She wanted to know what song it was, and she asked me, "Please, if you see me out, don't play that song again." She didn't want to relive the moment. But I said, "No. You let go. You released. That's what it's supposed to do. If I can get more of you all to release like that, then that's a powerful thing."

TOMMY:

This is why we're restricted. This is the power of dance and these cultures. The power to resist capitalism, conservatism, and normative behaviors. These dances can release us to a destiny that's not about solving commerce or a job, and that's very scary to the state. The state can't control us if we're all released.

BASS MATERIALISMS, MAROON CHOREOGRAPHIES, SONIC ECOLOGIES

Amid systems of domination, new modalities of resistance emerge, drawing strength from ancestral legacies of (re-)creation and in-/re-surgency. Black electronic dance musics represent forceful inheritors of Afro-diasporic traditions such as Vodou, Obeah, Hoodoo, and Candomblé. These spiritual practices, forged in the crucible of colonization, reclaimed rites of invisibility, intimacy, and ineffability as acts of defiance. Similarly, Black electronic dance musics diffract these rites through the ruptures and breakages of contemporary urban and digital soundscapes.

During the second half of the twentieth century, rhythm & blues and soul & funk gave way to drum & bass as the non-events of emancipation, desegregation, and decolonization yielded to the harsh realities of the "New Jim Crow," "Border Imperialism," and "Global Apartheid." These neo- and post-colonial racial capitalist apparatuses have reanimated and reinforced the analytics of coloniality and raciality—

anti-Blackness, slavery, and social death—through containerized logistics, just-in-time production lines, and digital identification and surveillance technologies. These systems seek to absorb billions of racialized subjects, fetishized objects, and commodified desires into a seamless im-/mobility regime, where every movement and interaction is synchronized in real time by machine intelligence. Arrayed against this meticulously orchestrated system of domination, Black electronic dance musics operate as fugitive modalities of resistance: their rhythms, improvisations, and sonic in-/re-surgencies counter the relentless abstraction and control of postmodern racial capitalism.

Through homological, analogical, and ecological kinships, Black electronic dance musics diffract Afro-diasporic rites of breakage and repair. Their layered rhythms, call-and-response relationalities, and subversions of societal hierarchies resound with those of Vodou, Candomblé, Hoodoo, and Obeah. They also transform sites of urban and digital decay into refuges of resistance, reviving maroon choreographies (fahima ife) that dismantle colonial hierarchies. Like Vodou's concealment within colonial Christianity, these musics hide radical potentials beneath the hedonistic entertainments, fostering connections to African roots while amplifying their fugitive possibilities.

As inheritors of Afro-diasporic sonic traditions, Black electronic dance musics reside within a continuum of innovation. From ragtime and jazz to dub and techno, they preserve the practice of layering rhythms to summon invisible forces and reclaim ineffable truths. To more effectively counter commodification and hypervisibility, however, these forms require intentional cultivation, sustaining their capacity to wield the break as a (re-)creative force. It is by embracing their invisible and ineffable dimensions that Black electronic dance musics are best realized as futurhythmachines, using sound to resist, survive, and reimagine communal entanglements.

THE BREAK AS MUSICAL, PSYCHOTHERAPEUTIC, AND SPIRITUAL PRINCIPLE

"The break" lies at the heart of Black electronic dance musics and countless Afro-diasporic traditions, embodying a rhythmic rupture and repair that exceeds sound to become a profound cultural and spiritual principle. Rooted in continental African musical practices, the break encapsulates the tension, disorientation, and transformation that define Black life and creativity under systemic oppression. This principle resonates with the fugitive erotics and diffractive kinships discussed earlier, where dismemberment becomes a (re-)generative force for confluence and renewal.

The persistence of the break across continental and diasporic African musics reflects homological, analogical, and ecological kinships that sustain cultural and spiritual significance. These dimensions of continuity and adaptation illuminate the break's centrality not only to music but also to the spiritual and psychotherapeutic practices that have nurtured Afro-diasporic (re-)creativity and resilience.

HOMOLOGICAL KINSHIP: RHYTHMIC CONTINUITIES FROM AFRICA
The break in Black electronic dance musics traces its roots to the polymetric and polyrhythmic traditions of African musics. African music thrives on the interplay of competing rhythms, creating a sonic tension in time(s) that resists the unified linear temporality imposed by Western musical logics. In Yoruba bātā drumming or Kongo ceremonial music, no single rhythm dominates; instead, participants negotiate overlapping patterns, crafting coherence out of temporal multiplicity and tension.

This rhythmic interplay underpins spiritual practices like Vodou drumming, where the layered rhythms facilitate spiritual possession, communal cohesion, and ecstatic states. Similarly, Afro-Brazilian Candomblé employs toques (drumming patterns) to summon orixás into sacred spaces, transforming rhythm into an act of resistance against colonial erasure. The break in Black electronic dance musics emerges as a homological continuation of these African rhythmic systems, preserved and reimagined across the diaspora to confront postmodern landscapes of racialized oppression and alienation.

ANALOGICAL KINSHIP: SYNCOPATION AND RESISTANCE

Diasporic syncopation exemplifies an analogical adaptation of African polyrhythms, shaped by the constraints of colonial and racialized oppression. Enslaved Africans reconfigured polyrhythms within the monorhythmic structures of Western music, producing syncopation as a tactical disruption. This rhythmic "compromise" not only allowed for survival within alien frameworks but also introduced defiant complexity, asserting Black agency within systems designed to suppress it.

In Black electronic dance musics, syncopated breaks—often implied "in the mix" and enacted by the dancer rather than fully realized in the track—extend the diffractions of diasporic existence, expressing both fracture and repair. Like the improvisational flows of jazz or the convulsive rhythms of funk, these breaks open portals for (re-)creation and renewal. As in Vodou ceremonies, where rhythmic rupture signals divine arrival, the breaks in Black electronic dance music summon spaces of communal defiance, ecstatic release, and collective transformation.

ECOLOGICAL KINSHIP: TRANSFORMING LANDSCAPES

Syncopation also represents an ecological symbiosis, where Afro-diasporic musics mimic, transform, and appropriate Western musical structures to ensure their own survival and dissemination. Like the orchid that mimics a bee to turn it into a pollinator, Afro-diasporic musics have deployed syncopation to repurpose monorhythmic Western forms as vehicles to spread polyrhythmic sensibilities globally.

Beyond this ecological mimicry, the break thrives by transforming cultural, technological, and spatial dynamics into sites of resistance. Black electronic dance musics reimagine warehouses, clubs, record stores, pirate radio transmitters, and digital platforms as refuges of rhythm, intimacy, and defiance, echoing the sacred ecologies of Vodou hounfō or Candomblé terreiros. These spaces serve as refuges where dismemberment—whether bodily, social, or historical—leads to the (re-)creation of flourishing relational and sensual fabrics.

Much like the African orchid's symbiosis with the bee, Black electronic dance musics appropriate and transform Western technologies—drum machines, sequencers, and samplers—and infuse them with African rhythmic logics. This adaptive interplay sustains cultural continuity while subverting systemic domination, following how Afro-diasporic rites have historically transformed oppressive conditions into fertile grounds for (re-)creation and resistance.

Genealogies of Sound and Spiritual Continuities

Black electronic dance musics are a transformative force within Afro-diasporic sonic traditions, embodying fugitive rhythms that weave together sound, relationality, and refuge. Like Haitian Vodou, North American Hoodoo, and Brazilian Candomblé, they transform dismemberment into collective communion, crafting spaces of fugitivity, intimacy, and resistance. Rooted in ritualized soundscapes, these spiritual practices navigated the violence of colonial modernity by turning rhythm into a means of survival and renewal. Similarly, Black electronic dance musics create immersive sonic ecologies that sustain Black life amidst systemic violence, while their fugitive erotic potential continues to evolve, reflecting deeper connections to the cultural and spiritual lineages that inform them.

The history of sound recording situates Black electronic dance musics within a continuum of Afro-diasporic innovation. As Michael Denning notes, the acoustic, electric, tape, and digital eras mark not only technological shifts but also changing socio-economic and spatial conditions for musical creation and experience. Afro-diasporic traditions adapted to these formations, preserving and reshaping polyrhythmic logics and communal resonance. Black electronic dance musics, as a distinctly digital phenomenon, extend this lineage by diffusing the polyrhythms of African music and the improvisational practices of Afro-diasporic rituals of breakage and repair.

THE ACOUSTIC ERA: RAGTIME & JAZZ

The acoustic era (1900–1920s) was defined by direct recording methods, where sound vibrations were captured on cylinders or discs through recording horns. Music was primarily circulated as printed sheet music, linking the parlor piano to live performances in vaudeville theaters and minstrel shows. Ragtime and jazz, emerging from this era, encoded African polyrhythms into the Western musical frameworks of sheet music and concert halls. These syncopated rhythms, much like Vodou's ritual drumming, employed breaks and improvisations as means to reclaim autonomy and conviviality from monomaniacal, monorhythmic systems of administration. But it was by putting oral and embodied traditions of improvisation into recorded grooves that this era laid the groundwork for later innovations in Black musical expression.

THE ELECTRIC ERA: RHYTHM & BLUES

The electric era (1920s–1950s) introduced microphones, loudspeakers, and amplified instruments, transforming sound into electrical signals for live performance, broadcasting, and recording. This era saw the rise of crooners and amplified instruments like the electric guitar, reshaping the intimacy and immediacy of musical experience. The microphone amplified subtleties previously imperceptible, reshaping vocal performance. Billie Holiday exemplified this shift with her ability to deliver whispered laments and piercing cries that drew listeners into her world, much like whispered Hoodoo incantations that carried transformative force. Rhythm and Blues extended this sacred energy into urban spaces, projecting rhythms in a manner that echoed the talking drums of Africa, compressing distances to engender greater erotic proximity.

The Tape Era: Soul & Funk

By the tape era of the mid-20th century, magnetic tape transformed music into a medium for layering and manipulation, enabling a new kind of sonic experimentation. Studios became laboratories of sound, where artists like George Clinton and Lee "Scratch" Perry layered rhythms and harmonies to create cosmic narratives that mirrored the celestial cosmologies of Vodou and Yoruba traditions. Clinton's *Mothership Connection* and Lee Perry's Black Ark both offered a mythological return to a spiritual homeland, reframing funk and dub, respectively, as vessels for radical and (re-)creative reparations. The hypnotic grooves of funk mirrored the trance-inducing rhythms of earlier Afro-diasporic rites, creating collective spaces of ecstasy and renewal on dancefloors and in listening rooms.

The Digital Era: Drum & Bass

The digital era that began in the late-twentieth century marked the reduction of sound into digital code, enabling infinite recombination and synthesis. Sampling became a defining feature, with recorded fragments transformed into new compositions. This practice recalls the bricolage of Hoodoo conjurers and the rhythmic layering of Vodou drummers. Drum machines, sequencers, synthesizers, and samplers became tools for constructing immersive dancefloors, echoing sacred ritual spaces where sound fosters communal intimacy and resilience. The digital tools of Black electronic dance musics, much like the chants and rhythms of Afro-diasporic spiritual traditions, transform historical fragments into technologies of liberation.

Sonic Ecologies and Fugitive Movements: Innovations Across Genres and Geographies

Black electronic dance musics thrive in the fertile tension between crisis and (re-)creation, where systems of oppression attempt to fragment Black life but instead sow the seeds of collective resistance. Like African and Afro-diasporic spiritual practices—Haitian Vodou's trance-inducing rhythms, Hoodoo's conjurations, and Candomblé's sacred dances—Black electronic dance musics transform trauma and displacement into sonic spaces of communion and defiance. Across sub-molecular (fleshy), molecular (relational), and molar (systemic) scales, Black electronic dance musics become spiritual technologies, weaponizing rhythm to assert Black vitality. From the towering soundsystems of Kingston to the frenetic pulses of singeli in Dar es Salaam, it crafts rituals of survival, transformation, and liberation.

KINGSTON'S SOUNDSYSTEMS: RITUALS OF SONIC POSSESSION (1960s–1970s)

Kingston's soundsystems echo African drumming traditions, summoning bodies into motion through bass-heavy vibrations that ripple through flesh and bone. These gatherings parallel the communal assemblies of Vodou *hounfò* and Candomblé *terreiros*, where rhythm restores fractured communal bonds. Soundsystems also repurpose discarded technology into forces of liberation, embodying Afro-diasporic practices of transforming colonial remnants into instruments of resilience. Globally, they disrupted cultural hierarchies, amplifying Jamaican innovations across the diaspora.

The Bronx's Breakbeats: Cyphers as Conjure Circles (1970s–1980s)

Hip-hop and electro-funk in the Bronx continue African polyrhythmic traditions, with breakbeats functioning as portals for transformation. These rhythmic disruptions mirror Vodou possession, channeling unseen forces into kinetic energy. In cyphers, dancers and MCs form circles of intimacy and collective power akin to Vodou possession dances or Candomblé rituals. On a systemic level, hip-hop subverted the culture industry, exposing inequities while affirming urban Black resilience.

House, Techno, and Jungle: Spaces of Creation and Defiance (1980s–1990s)

House music emerged from the abandoned warehouses of Chicago, where DJs turned industrial ruins into spaces of motion and connection. These gatherings were immersive, rhythmic sanctuaries that brought bodies together to reimagine the city's fractured, segregated landscapes. Techno, born in Detroit, reflected the city's postindustrial decline. Its stripped-down sound mirrored the emptiness of the Motor City, turning the absence of industrial vitality into a site for futuristic reinvention. Jungle arose from the reggae soundsystem clashes of London's tower blocks and council estates, layering rapid-fire rhythms and basslines that embodied the energy and tensions of diasporic life in urban Britain. These genres drew on their environments to transform spaces of decay and neglect into incubators of collective creativity and resistance.

FOOTWORK AND GRIME: CHOREOGRAPHIES OF RESISTANCE (1990s–2000s)

Chicago footwork's jagged, dismembered rhythms demand kinesthetic engagement, igniting competitive dance battles that transform bodies into vessels of resilience and renewal. Staged across the hyperghettoized South and West Sides—at abandoned warehouses, house parties, and even El train platforms—these performances fuse the improvisational spirit of Candomblé's trance-inducing rituals with the fluid, martial precision of Capoeira's choreographies. In London, grime's raw, minimalist soundscapes found amplification through the audacious tactics of pirate radio, broadcasting illegally from the rooftops of high-rise tower blocks while constantly relocating to evade detection. This nomadic defiance echoed Afro-diasporic spiritual practices that subverted colonial surveillance. Both genres reimagine urban landscapes as dynamic arenas of resistance, choreographing collective defiance and renewal through sound, movement, and community.

Singeli and Gqom: African Rhythms in Hyperdrive (2000s–2010s)

Singeli and gqom represent a forceful return of Afro-diasporic musical traditions to the African continent, a cyclical exchange of sound and spirit reminiscent of earlier waves of returns to the motherland. Just as Congolese rumba drew from Cuban rumba, Ghanaian highlife from American jazz, and Fela Kuti's Afrobeat from funk, singeli and gqom embody a synthesis of homological, analogical, and ecological kinships. These genres not only absorb Afro-diasporic influences but also reinterpret them within the context of contemporary African urban realities, contributing to the formation of an unprecedented planetary sonic ecology.

Homologically, the rapid tempos and layered polyrhythms of singeli and gqom draw from African musical traditions carried across the Atlantic by enslaved Africans, while resonating with diasporic forms like Chicago footwork and Detroit techno. Singeli retains ties to East African styles such as taarab and ngoma, while gqom's minimalist, bass-heavy sound reflects influences from Zulu isicathamiya, marabi, and reggae. These connections reveal how African polyrhythms, evolving across continents, gain new vitality in new forms.

Analogically, singeli and gqom also respond to the fractured realities of postcolonial urban life. Singeli channels the frenetic energy of Dar es Salaam's informal economies, much as jungle captured the tensions of Black British youth navigating systemic racism. Gqom's sparse, haunting beats parallel the structural inequalities of post-apartheid South Africa, where colonial legacies shape urban Black existence. Both genres turn these pressures into sonic expressions of resistance and renewal, reclaiming rhythm as a tool for survival.

Globally, singeli and gqom are evidence of a planetary sonic ecology shaped by racial capitalism's interconnected and integrated technosphere. Technologies such as containerized logistics and digital platforms simultaneously fragment communities and create cultural confluences. Black musical rites of breakage and repair mutate under these conditions, recombining traits from Afro-diasporic influences like hip-hop and house, while reentering global circuits to reshape and hybridize diasporic forms. Like Vodou's reanimation of Catholic iconography, they reanimate commodities of the culture industry in shared spaces of expression, reaffirming Afro-diasporic (re-)creativity as a force for resilience and entanglement.

The Pornoscopic Gaze and the Commodification of Black Electronic Dance Musics

Black electronic dance musics exist at the crossroads of rupture and repair, diffracting Afro-diasporic traditions of resistance and renewal. Yet, their liberatory energies are continually under siege from forces intent on commodifying and controlling them. Central to this commodification is the pornoscopic gaze—a colonial mode of seeing that renders Black creativity hypervisible, extractable, and subordinate to the analytics of coloniality and raciality

This gaze seeks to betray Black electronic dance musics in all senses of the word: exposing them to hostile systems of extraction, violating their intimacy and ineffability, and distorting their communal and spiritual functions. Through this betrayal, the pornoscopic gaze reframes these musics in alignment with the colonial order of sexuality, reducing their radical ecologies of sound and movement into consumable spectacles.

Spectacle and the Colonial Order of Sexuality

The colonial order of sexuality has long sought to subordinate Black cultural expressions by recasting them within narratives that serve hegemonic fantasies of Blackness as exotic, primitive, and dangerous.

Black electronic dance musics are no exception. Music videos, promotional campaigns, and curated festival aesthetics often privilege imagery that amplifies these narratives, foregrounding tropes of hypersexuality, uncontrolled primitive urges, and decadent excesses while erasing the layered complexities of the music's fugitive dimensions.

What were once maroon choreographies—collective rituals of defiance and entanglement forged in the crucibles of oppression—are reimagined as zones of voyeuristic consumption. The spaces where these musics once thrived as sites of intimacy and repair, such as clubs, warehouses, and house parties, are transformed into stages for the colonial gaze. Their hedonistic surfaces are exaggerated, detached from the histories and communities that sustain them, and commodified as visual aesthetics for broader consumption.

SOCIAL MEDIA AND SYMBOLIC ABSTRACTION

Social media platforms, integral to the technosphere of racial capitalism, intensify the pornoscopic abstraction of Black electronic dance musics. Algorithms favor content optimized for virality, privileging the fleeting spectacle over the immersive, relational, and sonic dimensions of the music. DJs, dancers, and producers are reimagined as influencers, their artistry disassembled into decontextualized fragments—

soundbites, clips, and images—crafted to cater to the insatiable demands of an easily distracted digital audience that craves titilation.

This process constitutes another layer of betrayal, where the improvisational, communal sonic ecologies of Black electronic dance musics are transformed into commodities circulating as cultural capital. The break—a sonic principle of rupture and repair that resists domination—is reduced to an aestheticized pause, repurposed for choreography challenges, memes, and lifestyle branding. By prioritizing hypervisibility, these platforms strip Black electronic dance musics of their ineffable and relational force, turning them into content detached from the cultural and historical matrices that produced them.

Complicity and the Filtering of Black Sound

This betrayal is not unidirectional. As with all systems of domination, racial capitalism exploits the drives of the flesh and the survival strategies of its subjects, drawing them into complicity. Black electronic dance musics, like other forms of Black cultural production, have at times been shaped by the demands of the culture industry, which extracts and repackages them for consumption by white middle-class audiences. As Orlando Patterson observed, these musics have been perverted to serve as a "Dionysian counterpoise" for the rigid Apollonian demands of a capitalist society rooted in Protestant work ethics, rationality, and efficiency.

Yet, the digestion of Black cultural production by white audiences is partial. As Aimé Césaire reminds us, the colonial culture industry consumes Blackness in the fashion of certain elementary types of digestive systems. "It filters. And the filter lets through only what can nourish the thick skin of its clear conscience." What the culture industry and its consumers absorb from Black electronic dance musics is only what can satisfy their Dionysian impulses—those stifled by corporate careerism, gentrified urban living, containerized logistics, and conformity to the colonial order of sexuality. This filtering process suppresses the music's radical, communal dimensions, allowing its consumers to enjoy the spectacle of Black creativity without confronting their own complicity in the systems that oppress Black communities.

RESISTING HYPERVISIBILITY AND COMMODIFICATION

Despite these betrayals, Black electronic dance musics retain their fugitive potential. As futurhythmachines, they remain capable of disrupting the logics of hypervisibility and commodification, reclaiming their role as tools of resistance and renewal. The break, central to their sonic and symbolic logic, continues to offersa template for refusal—a moment of rupture where abstraction is interrupted and relationality is reclaimed.

To preserve their radical possibilities, Black electronic dance musics must navigate the terrain of racial capitalism with greater intention and attention, fostering spaces where sound reclaims its invisible, ineffable, and intimate dimensions. These spaces must resist the distortions of the pornoscopic gaze, allowing the music to reassert its Afro-diasporic lineage as a force for maroonage, survival, and in-/re-surgence.

BLACK PLANETARY FUTURES

The break, central to Black electronic dance musics, is both a rhythmic principle and a portal—a vision of planetary futures forged through Afro-diasporic resistance and in-/re-surgence. Genres like singeli and gqom exemplify this, transforming dismembered histories into new continuities through the global circulation of sound. Created under the pressures of neo- and post-colonial racial capitalism—where containerized logistics, just-in-time production lines, and digital surveillance systems fragment Black life— these musics resist systemic erasure. Their beats (re-) connect and (re-)create diasporic communities, assembling invisible and ineffable forces into sonic ecologies that defy domination.

BASS MATERIALISMS: VIBE SHIFTS
Black electronic dance musics reclaim the flesh as a site of resistance, wielding basslines, subsonic vibrations, and dismembered rhythms to disrupt systems of control and commodification. Echoing Afro-diasporic traditions like Vodou drumming, where sound induces possession and vitality, these vibrations de-

stabilize the flesh's assimilation into polarizing bonds and molarizing systems. The bass conveys a fugitive force, a vibe that resists visibility.

Dreaming of futures rooted in rhythm, producers experiment with destabilizing frequencies, erratic amplitudes, and shifting tempos to subvert sensory norms. Like Hoodoo's ability to transform scraps into forces for liberation, these sonic experiments with sampled and synthesized breaks and loops encourage listeners to attune themselves to that which can be felt but not seen.

Maroon Choreographies: Pack Formations

Dancefloors are where fugitive bodies move together in improvisational rebellion, forging communizing bonds through shared rhythm. Like quilombos and the clandestine stations of the Underground Railroad, these spaces pulse with conviviality and hum with conspiracy, transforming collective movement into a unified force of (re-)connection, (re-)creation, and resistance. They are not merely zones of escape but dynamic grounds for entanglement and mutual care.

These spaces could develop their fugitive potentialities further, integrating mutual aid, communal education, and practices of (re-)creative repair, accentuating their role as refuges of radical praxis. Dancefloors might become laboratories for crafting new worlds, where communizing bonds deepen through shared movement and collective (re-)imagination, generating polyrhythmic pulses that not only escape but actively dismantle the boundaries imposed by coloniality and raciality, creating a space for communities to thrive together in shared purpose and resilience.

SONIC ECOLOGIES: MASS MOVEMENTS

Black electronic dance musics transform urban ruins and digital architectures into terrains of fugitivity. Clubs, warehouses, studios, and pirate radio frequencies become maroon infrastructures, where fragments of capitalist machinery are repurposed into tools for (re-)enchantment and subversion. These are riffs on Afro-diasporic rites, which have long transformed colonial ruins into sacred sites of repair.

In digital spaces, the possibilities widen: decentralized platforms become virtual *hounfò*, where rhythms flow across borders, producing planetary entanglements. The pulsations of a bassline might synchronize the urban sprawl of Kingston with the frenetic circuits of Dar es Salaam, connecting dancers, coders, and dreamers into a web of insurgent creativity. These digital platforms must be designed to resist centralization, mirroring the improvisational logic of Hoodoo's spells or Vodou's veves, where no pattern is ever fixed.

More-Than-Human Kinships

In dreaming these futures, Black electronic dance musics must deepen their resonance with non-human others. The vibrations of a subwoofer mimic the pulse of the earth, connecting dancers' movements to the rhythms of oceans, winds, and forests. A looped sample becomes a conversation with the mechanical hum of the urban, reconfigured as a collaborator rather than an oppressor. In such ways, Black electronic dance musics might better affirm a truth long understood by Afro-diasporic spiritualities: that life is not confined to human flesh but thrives in an intricate choreography of beings and forces.

Dancefloors can become part and parcel of the (re-)creation of sacred ecologies where humans and more-than-human entities repair and reimagine together—their vibrations inviting participants to move not just with one another but with the tides, the winds, and the deep bass of planetary rhythms.

From Breakdown to Breakthrough

The break is not merely a rupture; it is an aperture—an opening through which Black, Afro-diasporic life is scattered and transformed. Black electronic dance musics honor the fugitive erotics of the break, inheriting traditions of rhythmic resistance and improvisational repair. They invite us to listen, to move, and to sense futures where sound becomes an infrastructure of in-/re-surgence

The Black planetary futures suggested above are not prescriptions but invitations to deepen engagements with the kinships embedded in Afro-diasporic traditions. They envision rhythm, movement, and sound transforming ruins and fragments into refuges of renewal. Through the fugitive erotic power of the break, Black electronic dance musics suggest futures where Black life is able to thrive everywhere on this Earth, vibing with a more-than-human vitality.

POSTSCRIPT
Giving New Flesh to Old Wounds

"Who said that time heals all wounds? It would be better to say that time heals everything – except wounds. With time, the hurt of separation loses its real limits. With time, the desired body will soon disappear, and if the desiring body has already ceased to exist for the other, then what remains is a wound, disembodied."

—Chris Marker, *Sans Soleil*

In *The Anthropological Structures of Madness in Black Africa*, Alfâ Ibrâhîm Sow articulates a profound divergence from Eurocentric psychiatric paradigms. Within the confluent cultures comprising the Niger-Congo linguistic, psychic, and rhythmic continuum—and among societies shaped by its influence—madness is not perceived as an individual affliction or private pathology rooted in the self. Rather, the one marked by madness is recognized as a symptom, a signal akin to a canary in the coal mine, bearing witness to a deeper disorder borne by the entire social body. Their condition does not suggest an isolated psychic failure, but the first tremors of a collective affliction, reverberating across generations.

This trauma is not contemporary, but ancestral. According to Sow, Black Africa's ritual healers interpret madness as the expression of wounds sustained long ago—injuries inflicted upon ancestors that resound through time. The afflicted individual is not broken by what occurs in the present, but by what has been—by ancestral events that demand mourning, metabolization, and transfiguration again and again.

In this sense, the mad person resembles a vulnerable biome registering the early symptoms of anthropogenic climate collapse. The devastation unfolding in that biome was not caused by those living in the moment of breakdown, but by emissions and unsustainable decisions generations earlier. Likewise, the one marked by madness absorbs the renewed force of an ancestral catastrophe—its impact compounded and intensified through the passage of time.

Moreover, the collapse of the individual biome is not an isolated event but a harbinger of planetary crisis. Similarly, the collapse of the individual psyche signals a broader unraveling of the social fabric. The mad one does not stand apart from the body politic; they become its aperture, its exposed nerve. Their suffering is not only symptomatic. It is prophetic.

Madness, then, is not an ending but a recurrence—a looping, a re-sounding that disrupts linear chronologies and insists on return. Like the final lines of Finnegans Wake spiraling back to the book's opening, the wound refuses closure. It returns to the flesh not to vanish, but to demand reckoning anew. The afflicted body becomes a site where memory regains muscle, where submerged pain resurfaces as tremor, scream, rupture.

Within this cosmology, healing is not the sealing of the wound. It is not its erasure. Healing is its reanimation. As Joyce might put it, a commodius vicus of recirculation —a winding return through which the wound re-enters the world, not to be cured, but to be carried, redistributed, made legible across the body of the collective.

In this way, communal ritual becomes the means through which disembodied pain is re-embodied—not to end it, but to ensure it is held. Not so the wound may be forgotten, but so it may be shared. Through communal ritual, ancestral trauma is neither extinguished nor overcome, but transmitted—carried forward and diffused across the collective—so that all who belong to the social body might learn, together, how to bear what cannot be undone.

When one is struck by madness, it is not merely a private crisis. It is a public summons. The wound demands witnesses. Submerged trauma seeks a surface form. The affliction becomes an invocation—a call to communal ritual.

In this light, Black African ritual healers view Western psychology's isolation of the mad not merely as a misunderstanding, but as a harm. The pathologization, privatization, and institutionalization of suffering foreclose the wound's return to the collective flesh. They compel the sufferer to bear alone a burden meant to be shared. They deny the social body its opportunity to listen, to respond, to re-member.

Yet the healers know: this denial is not accidental. It is structural. Western civilization is founded on the systematic disembodiment of ancestral wounds—on the severing of people from lineages, cosmologies, and kinships. Nowhere has this been more violently enacted than in the case of the enslaved African and their descendants, who endured the most extreme forms of dispossession and rupture. But this severance did not end with emancipation. It persists as the enduring logic of Empire.

Even the colonizers, in their acts of conquest, mutilated their own psyches. Not by suffering wounds inflicted upon them, but by disavowing the wounds they inflicted. To wield colonial power required forgetting—again and again—what it cost.

What results is a civilizational madness masked as order. A collective affliction disavowed by the very systems that produce it. And so, the ghosts return. The wounds reappear. And ritual, once more, becomes necessary.

If communal ritual is the medium through which disembodied wounds are re-embodied—so they may be borne together—then history, unfolding in the wake of colonial catastrophe, demands a communal ritual response. The wounds we are called to carry are not only inherited; they are continually aggravated, salted daily by the machinery of Empire. And yet, as with those marked by madness, some among us are compelled to feel these wounds first—to tremble earliest, to absorb the shock of a world collapsing under the weight of its own contradictions.

Those of us who are able to sublimate the madness make art, do philosophy, write and recite poetry, organize noise—not to escape the wound, but to give it rhythm, to give it form, so that it may be shared. Our creations are not mere expressions; they are ritual objects, ritual mantras, ritual musics, and ritual myths. But rather than being received in acts of collective ritual, they are too often extracted from their ritual grounds, individualized, deritualized, institutionalized, and commodified—circulated as content, consumed as cultural artifact, trivialized as entertainment. In this way, the wound is exhibited but not embodied, displayed but not shared—rendered aesthetic in a manner that severs it from the social body meant to give new flesh to the old wound.

So, my provocation to you is this: how might we de-institutionalize, re-ritualize, and communalize our works—return them to the surround, the ritual ground where the wound might re-enter the world and be made legible across the body of the collective?

Signifying White Supremacy

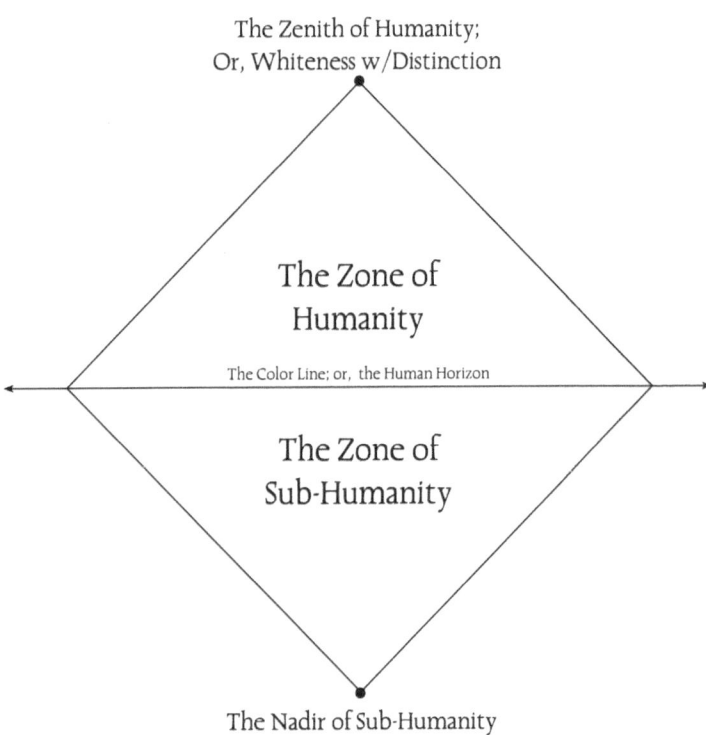

White supremacy positions whiteness with distinction—as the apex of humanity—at the furthest possible remove from Blackness without distinction, cast as the nadir of subhumanity. Whiteness guarantees inclusion within the Zone of Humanity, but it is whiteness marked by distinction—education, wealth, authority—that occupies its highest tier. In contrast, for Black people, distinctions may permit some elevation from the depths of subhumanity, but never full ascent to the apex. The ceiling remains fixed, no matter how high one climbs.

Signifying Anti-Blackness

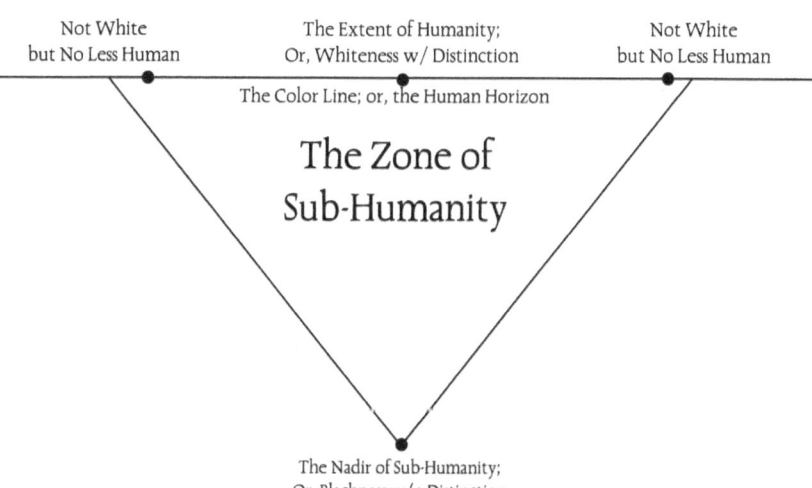

Anti-Blackness, by contrast, posits that whiteness with distinction is not the furthest point from Blackness without distinction, but rather the most direct—though treacherous—route from the depths of subhumanity to the threshold of the human. Unlike white supremacy, which structurally denies non-white ascent to the apex, anti-Blackness allows for the possibility of achieving parity with whiteness with distinction, but only through protracted, deferred trajectories. Still, Blackness without distinction remains fixed as the nadir of subhumanity—the basis against which humanity defines itself.

Signifying Radical Blackness

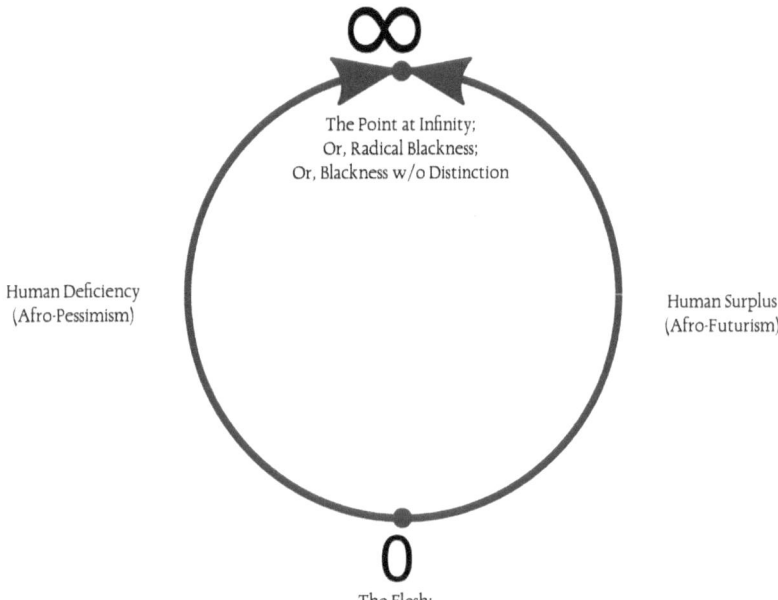

Radical Blackness rejects this fantasy of ascent altogether. It posits that the finish line has always already been reached—and undone. Blackness marks the point where the line curves back on itself, becoming a circle, a mathematical point at infinity. In projective geometry, the vanishing point at infinity is where parallel lines converge, a site where the visible slips into the unseen. In quantum field theory, infinities emerge when particles interact not just with their surroundings but with themselves, collapsing the boundaries between inter-action and intra-action, observer and observed. As metaphor, infinity invokes the invisibility, ineffability, and boundary-blurring intimacy of radical Blackness—a refusal to be fixed by surveillance or subsumed by control, existing in spaces where presence is no longer tethered to visibility, and where arrival is not the goal, but the disruption of the path itself.

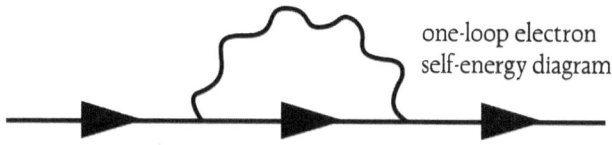

one-loop electron self-energy diagram

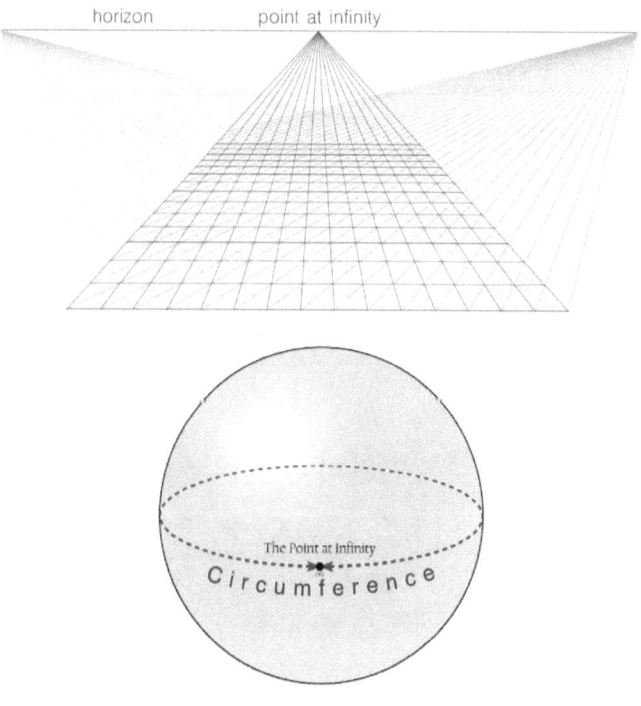

horizon point at infinity

The Point at Infinity
Circumference

www.ingramcontent.com/pod-product-compliance
Lightning Source LLC
LaVergne TN
LVHW041936070526
838199LV00051BA/2803